# TREASURE ISLAND
# & KIDNAPPED

W9-API-222

# NOTES

*including*
- *Life of the Author*
- *Lists of Characters*
- *Summaries*
- *Critical Interpretations*
- *Questions for Review*
- *Selected Bibliography*

*by*
*Gary Carey, M.A.*
*University of Colorado*

INCORPORATED

LINCOLN, NEBRASKA 68501

| Editor | Consulting Editor |
|---|---|
| *Gary Carey, M.A.* | *James L. Roberts, Ph.D.* |
| *University of Colorado* | *Department of English* |
| | *University of Nebraska* |

ISBN 0-8220-1306-1
© Copyright 1974
by
**Cliffs Notes, Inc.**
All Rights Reserved
Printed in U.S.A.

1997 Printing

Cliffs Notes, Inc.          Lincoln, Nebraska

# CONTENTS

# Life of the Author

Robert Louis Balfour Stevenson was born at Edinburgh, Scotland, on November 13, 1850. He was a sickly youth, but he did manage to attend school, where he did so well that he entered the university at sixteen. His family expected him to become a lighthouse engineer, but Robert preferred to study law. He was a young rebel; he thought that his parents' religion was an abomination and he soon became known as a bohemian, ranting against bourgeois hypocrisy.

When Stevenson was twenty-three, he developed a severe respiratory illness and was sent to the French Riviera to recuperate. This was the first of his many travels abroad, usually to France. In fact, many of his early writings use voyages and travels as their framework—*Treasure Island* and *Kidnapped,* for instance.

It was while Stevenson was staying at Fontainebleau in 1876 (he was twenty-six) that he met Fanny Osbourne, an American woman who was separated from her husband. He fell in love with her and, much to the horror of his parents, courted her for two years. In 1878, Mrs. Osbourne returned to California and the elder Stevensons felt that perhaps their son would come to his senses and forget the "loose" American woman. They were wrong. Robert decided to follow Fanny to California. He arrived there in 1879, very ill and very poor. It was not an easy time for the young lovers. Stevenson barely managed to eke out a living and was ill much of the time. They were married early in 1880 and, about the same time, they received a telegram from Stevenson's father, relenting and offering them financial support. Soon after their marriage, the couple sailed for Scotland.

For some time they lived in Switzerland because of Stevenson's health, but still he suffered bouts of illness; he returned to the Scottish Highlands, but was soon critically ill with a lung hemorrhage. He tried living in England, but the climate there was also bad for him. All this time, however, he was writing and publishing; *Treasure Island* and *Kidnapped* are both products of this period.

In August, 1887, Stevenson and his family sailed for America, where he found himself famous. Thus he chartered a yacht and sailed for the South Seas. He lived there for the rest of his life, writing novels, essays, and poetry and travelling among the islands. He died in Samoa in 1894. Surprisingly, his death was due to a cerebral hemorrhage, not the long-feared tuberculosis which had plagued him throughout his life.

# Treasure Island

## LIST OF CHARACTERS

**Jim Hawkins**

A young adventurer; he is largely responsible for averting the mutiny of the *Hispaniola* and for saving the lives of Dr. Livesey and Squire Trelawney.

**Mr. Hawkins**
**Mrs. Hawkins** } Jim's parents; they keep the Admiral Benbow Inn.

**Dr. Livesey**

A friend of the Hawkins family; a doctor and a magistrate, he is not afraid of the old sea captain who terrifies the Hawkins family and most of their guests.

**Squire Trelawney**

A tall man with a rough, red face. It is at his house where Jim and Dance find Livesey after Bones dies.

**Billy Bones**

A tall, heavy-set man, with a saber cut across one cheek, who appeared mysteriously one day at the Admiral Benbow with an old sea-chest.

**Black Dog**

A pale man, with two of his fingers missing. He quarrels with Bones and barely escapes with his life.

### Pew, the Blind Stranger

A surprisingly strong and nimble old man who gives the "black spot" to Bones. Moments later, Bones dies of apoplexy.

**Johnny**
**Dirk** } Comrades of Captain Flint.

### Mr. Dance

Chief revenue agent.

### Dogger

A revenue agent.

### Redruth

Squire Trelawney's gamekeeper.

### Blandly

An old friend of Trelawney, he secures the *Hispaniola* for the squire.

**Ben**
**Harry** } Two men in the Spy-glass who chase Black Dog.

### Morgan

Customer in the Spy-glass who drinks with Black Dog.

### Long John Silver

Cook on the *Hispaniola* who is nicknamed "Barbecue."

**Cap'n Flint**

Silver's parrot.

**Mr. Arrow**

An old sailor serving as mate aboard the *Hispaniola*.

**Captain Smollett**

Captain of the *Hispaniola;* a courageous, sharp-featured man.

**Job Anderson**

The boatswain aboard the *Hispaniola*.

**Israel Hands**

The coxswain aboard the *Hispaniola*.

**Abraham Gray**

One of the "honest sailors."

**Allardyce**

A corpse found on Treasure Island; he had served with Flint.

**George Merry**
**Tom Morgan**
**Dick**     Sailors aboard the *Hispaniola*.
**Alan**
**O'Brien**

**Ben Gunn**

One of Captain Flint's crew; he has been marooned for three years on Treasure Island.

# SUMMARIES

## PART I

### The Old Buccaneer

For a long time Jim Hawkins has been urged to write the story of what happened on Treasure Island. Finally he has decided to do so, telling everything except the location of the island.

When it all began, Jim's father managed the Admiral Benbow Inn on the seacoast of England. One day an old nut-brown sailor appeared, his hair pulled back in a pigtail, a scar across one cheek, and pulling a heavy sea-chest. He decided to stay at the Admiral Benbow after he learned that only a few people stayed there; he said that he was a captain and threw down several gold pieces as payment in advance for his room and board and rum. At first, he was a quiet man. During the day, Jim recalls, he watched the sea through a telescope and, at night, he drank rum and sat by the fire. He said little, usually asking only a single question: had any seafaring men been passing by? Whenever a sailor did stay at the inn, the old man would look at him through a curtained door before coming into the parlor. This was strange behavior, for sure, but Jim understood: the old man paid the boy a small sum of money each month if he would watch for "a seafaring man with one leg" and let him know the moment he appeared. Understandably, Jim had nightmares about the one-legged man.

Everyone at the inn, including the neighbors, was terrified of the old seaman. He was often drunk on rum, singing loudly and telling stories about hangings and wild deeds on the stormy seas. He used foul language and, although he scared the customers, they kept coming to the inn, fascinated by the excitement. The young people were especially fond of the old "sea dog"; to them, he was a "real old salt," the spirit of the mighty English navy. The captain stayed on, month after month, never paying any more money on his bill, knowing perhaps that Jim's father was afraid to ask for more gold coins.

Only one man ever confronted the captain. One night the old seaman was drunk and singing loudly when he suddenly yelled for silence in the inn. Everyone stopped except mild-mannered Dr. Livesey. Livesey kept talking in the same tone of voice, pausing to say that if the old sea captain kept drinking rum, the world would soon be rid of him. The captain threatened the doctor with a knife, but it was the captain who retreated finally, "grumbling like a beaten dog." The doctor left, saying that if there was a single complaint about the captain, he would have him hunted down. For many evenings after that, the inn was quiet.

Not long afterward, there occurred "the first of the mysterious events that rid us at last of the captain." It was a bitter cold winter; there were long, hard frosts and heavy gales. Jim's father was not well and Jim and his mother worked hard all day and evening.

One grey January morning, the captain was walking on the beach, his breath hanging like smoke. Jim's mother was upstairs with Jim's father when a tall, pale stranger entered the parlor; two fingers of his left hand were missing. He didn't seem to be a sailor, yet he had a sense of the sea about him. He asked for rum and also for "Bill," saying that the man whom he was looking for had a cut on one cheek. Thinking that the stranger was referring to the captain, Jim told him that the man was walking on the beach.

Jim was worried and watched the stranger, who was peering out the inn door like a cat waiting for a mouse. Jim himself stepped outside, but was roughly ordered inside and told to stand in the corner, behind the stranger.

The captain returned, saw the stranger, and stopped — looking as though he had seen a ghost. "Black Dog!" he said with a gasp. And Black Dog it was, come to see his old shipmate. Jim brought them rum and the two men talked for a long time. Suddenly there was a tremendous explosion. Chairs and tables were tipped over, and there was a clash of steel and a cry of pain. Black

Dog, with blood streaming from his left shoulder, disappeared in full flight over the edge of the hill.

The captain, reeling a little, demanded more rum. Jim was so shaken that he broke a glass when he heard a loud fall in the parlor. He ran and found the captain lying full length on the floor, his eyes closed and his face a horrible color. The boy tried to pour some rum down the captain's throat but was unable to. Luckily, Dr. Livesey arrived to visit Jim's father and was able to examine the captain. The old man, he said, had most likely had a stroke. He opened the captain's clothes and Jim was amazed by the tatoos on one of the man's great sinewy arms; he saw the name "Billy Bones" and a sketch of a gallows and a man hanging from it. The doctor then opened a vein and a great deal of blood gushed forth; finally the captain opened his eyes and asked about Black Dog. He was told that Black Dog had gone and the doctor warned him, once again, that one more drinking bout would kill him.

About noon, Jim stopped at the captain's door with a cooling drink and some medicine. The old man seemed weak, but excited. He told Jim that the one thing he needed was a drink of rum — despite the doctor's warning. He had lived on rum, he said. It had been his meat and drink and wife. If he didn't have a drink, he'd get the shakes and what he called "the horrors." Jim went for the rum, reluctantly, only because his father was ill and the captain was beginning to rant.

The rum fired the captain's spirits. He cried out that he would *not* stay in bed for a week. He threw back the blankets and tried to struggle out, but fell back, saying that Black Dog and his friends were after the sea-chest. He also ranted a great deal of seeming nonsense until, at length, he fell into a heavy sleep.

Jim's father died quite suddenly that evening and Jim was busy with the neighbors, arranging the funeral, and tending to the work of the inn. He scarcely had time to think of the captain. The captain, however, proved that, ill as he was, he could take care of himself. He came downstairs next morning and helped himself to the rum. The night before the funeral he was drunk as ever, singing and swearing loudly. Yet as weak as the captain was, everyone at the inn was very afraid of him, especially since Dr. Livesey was with a case many miles away.

The day of the funeral, Jim was standing in the door of the inn, looking out at the foggy, frosty afternoon, when he saw a stranger, plainly blind, tapping along the road with a stick, hunched over and wearing an old tattered sea-cloak with a hood. Jim went out to him, extended his hand, and was startled when the old stranger gripped it as tight as a vice. "Take me in to the captain," he said, "or I'll break your arm," wrenching it so fiercely that Jim cried out. Jim warned the old man that the captain was in a foul mood and usually had his cutlass drawn, but the blind stranger demanded to see him. Jim was so terrified that he obeyed.

The captain raised his eyes to the old man and looked not so much terrified as he did deathly sick. He too obeyed the blind man's demands, holding out his hand and receiving something in his palm, which he closed tightly. Moments later, he reeled, put his hand to his throat, swayed, and fell to the floor—dead.

Jim had to make some quick decisions. What was he to do? Ride for Dr. Livesey and leave his mother alone? What if Black Dog and the blind beggar returned for the sea-chest? What were they to do with the dead body of the captain on the parlor floor? He and his mother finally decided to leave together and, despite the gathering evening and the frosty fog, they ran to the next village for help. No one, however, was willing to return with them to the Admiral Benbow. Jim told of their troubles and referred to Captain Flint, a man whom the old captain had told of serving under as first mate. Obviously, the people had heard of Flint, even though Jim and his mother were not familiar with the name. At the mention of Flint, terror came to the men's eyes; they said they had seen strangers near the Benbow. They wanted no part of any trouble if it concerned Flint or any of his comrades.

Then Jim's mother shamed the men. She and her son would go back alone, she said. They were given a loaded pistol and one young lad offered to try and find Dr. Livesey.

Back at the Benbow, Jim bent over the captain's body, looking for the key to the chest, and discovered the "black spot," a piece of paper which read, "You have till ten to-night." The news, in a way, was good. It was only six o'clock. Jim cut the key, hanging from a piece of string around the dead man's neck, and he and his mother hurried upstairs and opened the chest. A strong smell of tobacco and tar filled the room. Looking into the chest, Jim saw a suit of clothes, clean and folded, some pistols, a bar of silver, an old Spanish watch, and several other trinkets. In the second layer, Jim's mother discovered a bundle, tied up in oilcloth, and a canvas bag that jingled as though it might be filled with gold. Perhaps there was a fortune in the chest, she said, but she would take only what was owed her—not a farthing more. The coins, Jim remembers, were of all sizes and from all countries.

They were about half-way through counting out what was due them when they both heard a noise—a blind man's stick tapping on the frozen road. Then the handle of the inn door was turned and the bolt was rattled loudly. After a while, there was silence.

Jim's mother jumped up and said that she would take what money she had; Jim grabbed the oilskin packet, and they fled into the night. They had not gone far, however, before they saw behind them, and rapidly advancing, a lantern tossing to and fro. Jim's mother fainted, but the young boy managed to drag her part-way under a bridge.

Like many boys, Jim was very curious and, despite his fear, he crept back up the bank and crouched behind a bush. He saw seven or eight men running toward the inn. There was a brief pause, then he heard them exclaiming that "Bill" was dead. Immediately they scattered upstairs and through the rooms looking for the chest. The cursing was fierce when they discovered that the chest had been opened. "It's these people of the inn—it's that boy," cried the blind man, "Scatter and find them!"

There was a whistle from far off, then another—a signal that warned the men of approaching danger. Within moments, there was the sound of horses galloping, a pistol shot, and the buccaneers separated in every direction. In the confusion, Pew (the blind man) was trampled to death. The horsemen proved to be revenue officers, summoned by the lad who rode for Dr. Livesey.

Jim and Mr. Dance, the chief revenue agent, returned to the Admiral Benbow and surveyed the destruction. Furniture had been thrown over and doors had been kicked in. Jim saw at once that he and his mother were ruined. The men were after money, he told Dance, but they were also after something else — the oilcloth packet containing the captain's papers, which he said he would give to Dr. Livesey.

Dance and Jim found Dr. Livesey at Squire Trelawney's, smoking a pipe and enjoying a bright fire. Dance told him what had happened and Jim showed Dr. Livesey the oilskin packet, which he pocketed. After Dance left, Dr. Livesey and the squire discussed Captain Flint, a man they described as "the bloodthirstiest buccaneer that sailed." Then Dr. Livesey questioned the squire: "Supposing that I have here in my pocket some clue to where Flint buried his treasure, will that treasure amount to much?"

The squire said that Flint's treasure would be so great that the squire himself would outfit a ship and search for it. The doctor was satisfied and opened the packet. Inside he found two things — a book and a sealed paper. The book contained sailing notations and amounts of money, recorded over nearly twenty years, with crosses denoting the names of ships sank or towns plundered. The sealed paper contained a map of an island about nine miles long and five across, with two harbors and a hill in the center. On the island were three crosses of red ink — two on the north part of the island and one in the southwest; on the latter, in small, neat handwriting, was the notation "bulk of the treasure here." On the back of the map was further information.

Dr. Livesey and the squire were filled with delight. Tomorrow they would start for Bristol and in ten days they would be ready to sail, with young Jim Hawkins as cabin-boy.

Dr. Livesey, however, became suddenly serious. The squire had a loose tongue—he must tell *no one* of their plans. He must arrange for the ship and, just before they were ready to sail, Dr. Livesey and Jim would join him. If the buccaneers were to hear about the map, they would be ruthless. The squire promised to be as silent as a grave.

## PART II

### The Sea-Cook

It took much longer than the squire thought for the ship to be outfitted and ready for sea. In the meantime, Livesey went to London to attend to medical matters and Jim stayed at the Hall, Squire Trelawney's estate, under the charge of old Redruth, Trelawney's gamekeeper. The weeks passed on until a letter arrived from Trelawney, describing the *Hispaniola* and describing Long John Silver, the man whom Trelawney had hired to serve as cook on the ship. He also said that Hawkins should bid his mother good-bye and come at once to Bristol. Jim was excited by the letter but was troubled by one sentence; Trelawney said that everyone in Bristol worked hard to outfit the ship "as soon as they got wind of the port we sailed for—treasure, I mean." The squire had revealed their secret—the buried treasure—the very thing Dr. Livesey warned him against.

Young Hawkins and Redruth returned to the Admiral Benbow and were happy to find Jim's mother in good health and the inn in fine shape—the latter due to the squire's generosity. In addition, the squire had hired a young boy to help Jim's mother manage the inn. Jim felt close to tears, but on the following day he and Redruth were on the road again, arriving soon in Bristol after hailing a passing mail coach. The two walked along the docks, marveling at the great multitude of ships of all sizes and nations. Soon Jim himself would be aboard one of these schooners, bound for an unknown island to seek buried treasure! He was in this intoxicating dream when he reached the far end of the dock and met Squire Trelawney, who was overjoyed to see his young cabin-boy. At last the ship's company was complete. Tomorrow they would sail.

After breakfast, Squire Trelawney asked Hawkins to deliver a note to John Silver at the Spy-glass, a tavern on the docks. Silver was quickly recognized: he was a tall and strong man whose left leg was cut off close by the hip; he walked with a crutch under his left shoulder. He was whistling as he moved among the guests of his inn, greeting old favorites. Jim felt relieved; he had feared that Silver might prove to be the one-legged sailor whom the old captain had feared. As an introduction, he handed the innkeeper Squire Trelawney's note and, a moment afterward, he saw a familiar fellow dash out the door — it was Black Dog! Silver ordered a man after him and asked Morgan, who had been drinking with Black Dog, what he knew about him. Morgan claimed that the man was a stranger. Jim, however, became suspicious of Silver — then he dismissed the matter, especially after Silver began to laugh at the man's escaping — and his failing to pay for his rum. "Shiver my timbers," he roared, saying that because of his own incompetence that he — and not Hawkins — should be the cabin-boy.

Silver joined Jim on the quay and as they returned to Squire Trelawney, he told the boy about the different ships they looked at, plus many anecdotes of ships and seamen, coloring his talk with nautical phrases. To young Jim Hawkins, Silver seemed to be the best of all possible shipmates.

Shortly thereafter, Jim, Dr. Livesey, and Squire Trelawney boarded the ship and were hardly in the squire's cabin when a sailor announced that Captain Smollett wanted to see the squire.

The captain proved to be most outspoken: he had been engaged on "sealed orders" and now that he knew that they were going on a treasure hunt, he didn't like the plan; in addition, he didn't like the crew — any of them. Further, he didn't approve of the crew's putting powder and arms in the fore hold; powder and arms should be stored under the cabin. He had also heard that the squire had a map of an island with crosses on the map to show where the treasure was — and then he described the exact latitude and longitude of the island. Squire Trelawney was shaken, saying that he told no one of the location. Neither Dr.

Livesey nor Hawkins, however, paid much regard to the squire's protestations. The captain left, then, agreeing to stay in his position, and Dr. Livesey commented that he felt that there were two honest men in the crew — the captain and John Silver. The squire disagreed. He believed the captain to be unmanly, unsailorly, and downright un-English.

There was a great deal of work to be done before the voyage began. Many things had to be stowed in their places and boatfuls of the squire's friends came to wish him a good voyage and a safe return. Little wonder that young Jim Hawkins was dog-tired when, a little before dawn, he heard the boatswain sound his whistle, saw the crew begin to man the capstan-bars, and listened with awe to Silver singing the song sung so often by the dead sea captain:

> "Fifteen men on the Dead Man's Chest —
> Yo-ho-ho, and a bottle of rum!"

Soon the anchor was alongside the bows, the sails were drawn, and land and ships were flitting by on either side. The *Hispaniola* had begun her voyage to the Isle of Treasure.

The trip was generally pleasant except for two or three things. Mr. Arrow was a poor authoritarian and after a day or two at sea, he often had to be ordered below deck because of drunkenness; strangely, no one knew where he got his liquor or ever saw him take a drink. Nobody was much surprised nor very sorry when one dark night he, they assumed, fell overboard.

In contrast, all the sailors admired and liked Long John Silver or, as they nicknamed him, "Barbecue." Hawkins was especially fond of him and Silver was always kind to Hawkins, and was always glad to see him in the galley, which he kept clean and neat. Jim was also fond of Cap'n Flint, Silver's parrot, which he kept in a cage in one corner. Cap'n Flint was quite a talker and often said, over and over, "Pieces of eight! pieces of eight! pieces of eight!" until Jim wondered why the bird was not out of breath. Silver enjoyed talking about the bird, saying it was probably two hundred years old and had seen more wickedness than the devil himself.

The squire and Captain Smollett continued to be on distant terms, but the *Hispaniola* itself proved to be an able ship, easily riding through heavy weather. As for the crew, they were spoiled, getting double the booze ration for the least excuse and there was always a barrel of apples for any one to help himself to. The captain was especially unhappy with the apple barrel. Yet, as Jim says, the apple barrel was a blessing in disguise, for the day before they sighted the island, Jim got into the barrel, found it almost empty, and, dozing, suddenly heard Silver's voice. What he heard frightened him. He was convinced that the lives of all the honest men aboard were in danger.

Silver's words were indeed fearsome: he had served under the infamous Captain Flint and spoke of himself as a "gentleman of fortune." It was not long, however, before Jim realized that the term was synonymous with "pirate." Israel Hands was anxious to mutiny immediately; he wanted the captain's pickles and wine. Silver quieted him. He himself would give the word, but not until the squire and the doctor found the buried treasure, got it aboard, and Smollett had navigated the ship half-way back. Once the mutiny was accomplished, Silver said, he would kill those who were not with him — with one condition. Silver wanted Squire Trelawney himself; he wanted to "wring his calf's head off his body." Then, suddenly, he asked Dick to fetch him an apple.

Jim panicked and, a moment before Dick reached into the barrel, Hands suggested that they all have a drink. The men went to get their rum and Jim sat in the barrel, shaking and looking at the moon. Wondering what he should do, he was startled to hear the voice of the lookout shouting "Land ho!"

Quickly he leaped from the barrel, raced to the open deck, and joined Hunter and Dr. Livesey. To the southwest were two low hills and behind one of them a higher hill, whose peak was buried in fog. The captain inquired if any of the men had seen

that particular island before. Silver answered that he had and
that the island was called Skeleton Island; he said further that it
was believed to be a stopping-place for pirates. The tallest hill
was called Spy-glass. Jim was amazed at Silver's coolness, even
to confessing knowledge of the island. He shivered when the
cook laid a hand on his arm, describing the many trees to be
climbed on the island and the goats they would hunt.

As soon as he was able, Jim was quick to tell Dr. Livesey that
he had something terrible to relate to the captain and the squire.
Before long, he was summoned to the captain's cabin. Dr.
Livesey and Squire Trelawney were also there. The boy told
what he heard in the apple barrel. They poured him a glass of
wine and the squire confessed that he had indeed been an ass.
The captain confessed that he had likewise been duped, but he
had a plan: they must go on. Were they to turn back now, Silver
would call for a mutiny. They would wait and "some fine day"
they themselves would attack when Silver and his friends least
expected it.

## PART III

### My Shore Adventure

Next morning when Hawkins came on deck, the island
looked altogether different. Grey-colored woods covered most
of it and the tallest hill, Spy-glass, rose up from almost every
side, then was suddenly cut off at the top like a pedestal to put a
statue on. He recalls that the ship was rolling that morning and
he had to cling tight to the backstay; he had always been a good
enough sailor, he tells us, but he never learned to stand on a rolling ship—on an empty stomach—without getting a touch of sea-
sickness.

From the first, Jim hated the very thought of Treasure Island.
It was grey and melancholy and had steep beaches; it was un-
inviting and he was not anxious, as he had thought he would be,
to leave the ship.

There was much work to be done: there was no wind and the boats had to be manned and the ship warped three or four miles round the corner of the island and up a narrow passage. The heat was sweltering and all the men were grumbling – all except Silver. Long John, it was obvious to Jim, knew the passage like the palm of his hand. There was not a sound except the surf booming half a mile away. A peculiar stagnant smell hung over the spot where they anchored.

Long John worked, perhaps, hardest of all that morning, going from group to group, giving friendly advice, outstripping himself in civility.

The captain was quick to call a council of his friends. The mood of the ship, he said, was bad, but his plan was this: he would allow the men an afternoon ashore – on their own. Loaded pistols would be given to the men whom the captain felt were loyal; these included Hunter, Joyce, and Redruth.

When shore leave was announced, the men scattered like wild animals, thinking they might find the treasure as soon as they were on land. The captain allowed Silver command of the landing and it was plain that Silver was indeed clever; he left six men behind on the ship. Thus the honest men, numbering six, were probably powerless to take and fight for the ship.

Suddenly it occurred to Jim to go ashore; he slipped over the side and curled up in the nearest boat as she shoved off. As it happened, Jim's boat struck the shoreside trees, but Jim was able to catch a branch, swing himself out, and plunge into the nearest thicket. Silver yelled at him, but Jim paid no heed. He ran until he could run no longer.

Having given Long John the slip, Hawkins began to explore the strange island. He crossed a marshy area and came out on an open piece of sandy country dotted with pale contorted trees. On the far side stood one of the hills. For the first time he felt the joy of exploration – the exhilaration of being alone, discovering unknown flowering plants, and listening to the noises of strange birds.

He passed through a thicket of oak-like trees and reached a marsh, steaming in the strong sun, and, through the haze he was able to see Spy-glass. He gazed at it for only a moment, for all at once a duck flew up, and soon, over the whole surface of the marsh, a cloud of birds hung screaming and circling. And there was also another noise — the low tone of human voices.

Jim began crawling on all-fours, steadily and slowly, toward the voices until he could see two of the crew — Long John Silver and Tom, one of the honest sailors. Silver seemed to be threatening the fellow. Jim bent forward to listen and heard a sudden cry, then one horrid, long-drawn scream. Silver did not flinch; he told Tom that the noise was probably Alan (another honest sailor). At this, Tom became defiant; he refused to join Silver's band of men; he turned and began to walk away, but he did not go far. Silver seized a branch and hurled it with a violent crunch between Tom's shoulders. The sailor fell and before he had time to rise, Silver had buried his knife twice in Tom's body.

Jim felt faint; the birds and the tall Spy-glass hilltop whirled round and round and bells rang in his ears. He heard Silver blow several blasts on a pocket-whistle and guessed that he was calling his men. Instantly he began crawling back through the thicket. He had never known such fear. Would he too be killed if he were discovered? Would he find the squire and the doctor and the captain dead? He paused at the foot of the little hill with two peaks.

Something moved. A figure — a bear, a man, or perhaps a monkey — leaped behind a pine tree. Was this the end? Behind Jim were murderers; before him some unknown thing was lurking. He decided to take his chances with Silver and turned in the direction of the boats.

The figure flitted like a deer, running from tree to tree, trying to head the boy off. Jim wondered if it might be a cannibal, for it ran on two legs, yet was unlike any man he'd ever seen. Remembering that he had a pistol, Jim started toward the man and, to his wonder and confusion, saw the man race toward him and throw himself on his knees, holding out his clasped hands in supplication.

The man said that he was Ben Gunn and that Jim was "the first Christian" he had spoken to in three years. Gunn was deeply browned, his lips almost black; he was dressed in old canvas rags, held together by odd brass buttons and bits of stick. He had not been shipwrecked, he told the boy, he was marooned and had lived on goats and berries and oysters. He asked, first of all, for what he desired most in the world: a piece of cheese. He said that for three years he had dreamed of cheese (toasted, mostly). Then he told Jim something surprising—Gunn was a rich man. Furthermore, because Jim had found him, Gunn would make Jim a rich man. A shadow crossed his face: did the ship anchored in the harbor belong to Flint? Jim explained that Flint was dead, but that some of Flint's crew were aboard, including a one-legged man—Long John Silver, a name Gunn knew well.

Jim told Gunn the story of their voyage and about their predicament and Gunn listened keenly. He agreed to aid the boy and hoped that the squire would be generous, in exchange for Gunn's help. Jim assured him that the squire was a fair-minded man, and Gunn, in turn, confessed that he was on Flint's ship when Flint and six seamen buried a vast treasure. Flint and the men were on shore for a week, Gunn recalled, and when he returned, he was alone: Silver had killed the seamen and buried them. Billy Bones was the mate on that ship and Long John Silver was the quartermaster. That was years ago.

Then, three years ago, Gunn was on another ship and convinced the crew to search the island for Flint's treasure. For twelve days they looked for it; finally they disgustedly gave up and handed Gunn a spade and a pickax and told him to find the treasure himself. Then they sailed away. But, said Gunn, he did not panic. He built a small boat, which could now be used to take them to the *Hispaniola*. As he was talking, the island echoed with the thunder of a cannon and, after a considerable interval, a volley of small arms.

"They have begun to fight," Jim said.

The two began to run, then paused; not more than a quarter of a mile in front of them, a flag — the Union Jack — fluttered in the air.

## PART IV

### The Stockade

The narrative in the first part of this section of the novel is continued by Dr. Livesey. It was about half past one, he recalls, when the two boats went ashore from the *Hispaniola*. He and the squire and the captain were talking matters over when Hunter came down with the news that Hawkins had slipped into one of the boats and gone ashore. It was bad news. Knowing the temper of the crew, Dr. Livesey wondered if they would ever see the boy again.

Before long, Hunter and Livesey became impatient and decided to go ashore. They pulled straight in and the two men guarding Silver's boats seemed alarmed when they saw the doctor and Hunter, but they did not leave their posts. Livesey steered the boat around the coast, out of sight, and jumped out, his pistols cocked. He had not gone a hundred yards, however, before he discovered the stockade.

The structure was superbly constructed. It sat on a knoll and was made of stout logs and was large enough to hold forty people. Around it, the land had been cleared. Whoever controlled the stockade was safe, could sit quietly and shoot would-be invaders like partridges. But what was particularly pleasing to Livesey was the fact that spring water flowed from the knoll; the one thing lacking on the *Hispaniola* was fresh water.

He was thinking this over when he heard a cry of violent death. "Jim Hawkins is gone" was his first thought. Within minutes, Dr. Livesey was back in the boat and soon he and Hunter were alongside the schooner. He found the squire white as a sheet. The captain was not shaken, however, and listened eagerly to Dr. Livesey's plan. The men positioned themselves at critical points, with several loaded muskets, then Hunter brought a boat around and began loading it with food, ammunition, and medicine. When they were finished, the captain hailed Israel Hands, telling him that if any of Silver's henchmen made a move, they would be shot. Then Joyce and Livesey made for shore. Again Silver's lookouts were alarmed as they saw the boat disappear around the bend.

After several boatloads of provisions were stowed in the stockade, the men risked a final load of supplies, dumping the rest of the arms and powder overboard and picking up Redruth, the captain, and Abraham Gray.

This final trip was not an easy one. The little jolly-boat, as it was called, was gravely overloaded. It carried five grown men and far too many supplies. Water began seeping in and, in addition, the tide was taking them from the landing place behind the bend. They were in danger of docking beside Silver's boats, yet could not steer any stronger because they might swamp the boat. No one dared breathe.

When the captain spoke, his words were heavy: they had forgotten the cannon on the ship and, looking back, they saw Silver's men taking off the tarpaulin cover. Another matter was also forgotten: Israel Hands had served as Flint's gunner. They were as easy a target as a barn door.

The captain ordered Trelawney to fire at the sailors — Hands, if possible. He did so, missed Hands, but fell one of the other seamen. Onshore, the pirates came running out from among the trees. The squire tried another shot but this time the jolly-boat lurched and sank, gently, in three feet of water. Luckily, however, two of their five guns were saved. Livesey held his over his head and the captain managed to keep his dry. They waded ashore as fast as they could, hoping that Hunter and Joyce had managed to hold the stockade.

Racing toward the stockade, they heard footfalls and the cracking of branches behind them. They ran for the south side of the stockade and as they reached it, seven mutineers appeared at the southwestern corner. Hunter and Joyce scattered six of the men with a volley of shots and one fell dead. In the skirmish, Redruth was shot and was carried, groaning and bleeding, into the log house.

In the meantime, the captain found a long fir tree and, with the help of Hunter, he used it for a flag pole and ran up the Union Jack. He then consoled the squire and conferred with Dr. Livesey. They had sufficient powder and shot, but rations were short; perhaps, he said, it was fortunate that Redruth had been killed.

No sooner had the captain made his observation than a cannon ball passed overhead. The squire suggested taking down the flag; after all, the mutineers could not see the stockade and were aiming for the flag. The captain was adamant: the flag was to remain up and show their strong resolve to the enemies.

All evening long, ball after ball landed near or inside the enclosure but, as Dr. Livesey says, "we soon got used to that sort of horse-play and minded it no more than cricket." And so the captain sat down to his log, entering the events of the day, recording Redruth's death and, about to register the supposed fate of young Jim Hawkins — Hawkins himself appeared, safe and sound, climbing over the stockade wall.

The narrative at this point is resumed by Hawkins.

Ben Gunn, he says, was relieved to see the British flag. Were Silver inside the stockade, the Jolly Roger would have been flying from the fir tree. Jim was eager to rejoin his friends but Ben detained him a moment, explaining that he was going back to the place where Jim had found him. If the squire agreed to help Gunn, Hawkins could come for him. Jim agreed and when a cannon ball landed less than a hundred yards away, Gunn took flight.

Jim had a difficult time getting into the stockade. The balls peppered the area, so he crept down among the trees along the shore where he could see the *Hispaniola*. Flying from her peak was the black flag of piracy—the Jolly Roger. When at last he was able to get into the stockade, he was warmly welcomed and quickly related what had happened to him. His friends listened carefully, then divided the party into watches. Jim was stationed at the door as their sentry. From time to time the doctor came to the door for a little air and, on one of those occasions, he and Jim talked about Ben Gunn. If the fellow did indeed like cheese, said Livesey, then he would have cheese. Livesey well understood this fancy of Gunn's, for, he said, he always carried (as his private comfort) a goodly portion of Parmesan cheese in his snuff-box.

Before supper, old Tom was buried. Then the men ate a meal of pork, drank some strong brandy, and discussed their prospects. Their best hope seemed to be to kill off the buccaneers as soon as possible. Every time they took a shot at them, they were to aim with extremest care. From about half a mile away they could hear the enemy roaring and singing. Jim fell asleep quickly that night and slept well into the morning, rousing only after he heard some one exclaiming, "Flag of truce!" He looked out. It was Long John Silver.

Two men were outside the stockade and, indeed, one was Silver, standing in knee-deep vapor fog. The captain warned his men about this being a trick, then went to the porch. Silver explained, humbly, that the men chose him captain after Smollet's "desertion" and that he wanted to talk with Smollett. Smollett agreed and Silver made his way, though not without some difficulty up the knoll. What he had to tell the captain was puzzling— to everyone except Jim, who guessed that it was Gunn who sneaked into the enemy camp during the night and killed one of the men. Now the "honest sailors" had only fourteen buccaneers to deal with.

Silver's mission was simple: he wanted the treasure map. The terms, he said, were also simple. In exchange for the map, Smollett and his men had a choice: they could come aboard the *Hispaniola*, once the treasure was loaded (Silver gave his word

that they would arrive safe ashore) or they could divide the treasure among all the men and Silver would hail the first passing
ship and send them to pick up Smollett and his men.

The captain then offered Silver a choice: either Silver and
his men come up one by one, unarmed, allow themselves to be
clapped in irons and taken home for a fair trial in England—or
Silver's crew would wind up at the bottom of the sea.

Before he left, Silver spit into the spring and, with a dread-
ful oath, he stumbled off, disappearing among the trees.

The captain roared for his men to return to their sentry posts
and warned them that within the hour they could expect an attack from Silver's party. He offered Hawkins a bite of breakfast
and told Hunter to serve a round of brandy to them all. An hour
passed. The men strained their eyes and ears. Suddenly Joyce
fired and was answered by a volley of shots from every side of
the enclosure. Shortly, a little cloud of pirates leaped from the
woods and swarmed over the fence. Squire and Gray fired and
three men fell. Four of the pirates, however, ran straight for the
building. The situation was utterly reversed. The log house was
full of smoke and filled with cries and confusion. Jim grabbed a
cutlass and sent one of the mutineers sprawling, a great slash
across his face.

Soon nothing remained of the attacking party, but when he,
the doctor, Gray, and Jim returned to the house, they found
Hunter, stunned, and Joyce, shot through the head. The squire
was supporting the captain, one as pale as the other.

## PART V

### My Sea Adventure

Since the mutineers did not return, Trelawney and Hawkins
used the quiet time to fix some food while the doctor tended to
the wounded. Hunter never regained consciousness, but the
captain was in better shape. One of the shots had broken his

shoulder blade and had touched a lung; the other had torn some muscles in the calf, but none of his organs were dangerously injured. He was sure to recover, according to Dr. Livesey, if he did not walk, move excessively, or speak, if he could help it.

After a long consultation with the squire, Livesey left. Jim envied the doctor's freedom. The late afternoon heat in the house was stifling and the dead bodies lying all around were disgusting. Rashly he filled his pockets with biscuits and, seeing that no one was observing him, grabbed a brace of pistols and stole out of the stockade. He headed for the east coast of the island where he hoped to find the white rock that Ben Gunn had mentioned. If he could find it, perhaps he could ascertain where Gunn had hidden his boat.

When Jim reached the shore, he walked leisurely beside the surf, then crept warily up the ridge. There was the *Hispaniola* and in one of the boats alongside was Silver and several men, talking and laughing. Noticing that the sun was low, the boy headed for the white rock. Night had almost come when he reached it and, below it, hidden in knee-deep undergrowth was a goatskin tent; inside, he found Gunn's boat. The temptation for more adventure was too great—Jim decided to use the boat to slip out to the *Hispaniola* and cut her loose. He waited until it was absolutely dark, then shouldered the small boat and, wading a little way in, he set it down on the surface.

Gunn's boat (a "coracle," Jim calls it) seemed quite safe, but she was a most lopsided craft to manage, tending to turn round and round however Jim steered her. Most of the time he seemed to be rowing broadside. With luck and a good tide, he reached the *Hispaniola* and laid hold of her hawser, which was as tight as a bowstring. A fearful thought occurred to him: if he were to cut the hawser, the ship would rock so violently that he and Gunn's ship would probably be tossed high out of the water. Fortune, however, came to Jim's aid. Southerly winds caught the ship and forced her into the current; to Jim's joy and relief, he felt the hawser slacken. Quickly he jerked out his knife and began to cut the anchor's rope. When he was almost finished, he paused for a moment, listening to the angry, drunken voices of Israel Hands and another seaman. The breeze came again, Jim felt the hawser slacken once more and, with a good slice, he cut the last fibers through.

The *Hispaniola* began to turn, spinning slowly, shoving the coracle ahead of her. At length, it was free of the schooner but when a light cord trailed across Jim's hand, he grabbed it, impulsively. He felt especially courageous and curious and so he pulled himself up, hand over hand, until he could peer in the window of the ship. Satisfied that Hands and his comrade were drunk, he dropped back into the little skiff. Meanwhile, the current had turned the schooner and sent it and the coracle out toward the open sea.

It seemed hours that Jim lay in the bottom of the boat and, gradually, he grew weary; finally, he fell asleep, dreaming of home and the old Admiral Benbow.

When Jim awoke, he found himself tossing at the southwest end of Treasure Island. Fortunately he was only out about a quarter of a mile and his first thought was to paddle in. But that notion was quickly rejected. The breakers were spouting and heavy sprays were flying. Jim could imagine too easily being dashed to death on the craggy shore. And there was something else: sea lions, barking and crawling, were scattered on the flat expanses of rock.

Jim decided to take his chances with the sea, using the current to head northward. He soon found that he was unable to paddle, so he lay in the boat watching the waves, which looked like silvery ranges of hills and valleys. When he passed a cool-looking line of green tree-tops, he became almost sick with longing and thirst. He ached for water and was feeling pitiful indeed when he was carried past the point and—not half a mile away— he sighted the *Hispaniola*. He scarcely knew what to feel for a moment, then he noticed something odd: the ship was sailing by swoops and dashes; her sails were idly flapping. Obviously no one was steering her. Where were the crew? Were they drunk or had they deserted her?

The thought of boarding the ship inspired Jim. He tried with all his strength and caution to paddle the coracle and was soon gaining on the schooner. Still no one appeared on deck. When she came around broadside, Jim acted fast. He was on the summit of one swell and the schooner was on another. With one hand he caught and pulled himself up the jib-boom. Looking down, he saw the schooner strike the coracle. He was stranded on the *Hispaniola!*

The canvas sails crackled like cannons, nearly tossing Jim into the sea, but he regained his balance and tumbled headfirst onto the deck. Not a soul was to be seen—only an empty bottle, tumbling to and fro. Then he saw the bodies: the red-capped watchman, lying dead, crucifix-like, and, near him, Israel Hands, propped against the bulwarks, his face white as a sheet. The ship bucked and slid and, as it did, the red-capped corpse slipped to and fro. Hands seemed to sink and settle, each time a little more, onto the deck. Around both of them were splashes of dark blood.

While Jim stood looking and wondering what to do, Hands gave out a low moan and writhed upward. He uttered a single word: "Brandy." The boy raced down to the captain's cabin, dodging the dozens of empty bottles clinking together. At last he found a bottle with some brandy in it and, for himself, he grabbed a biscuit and a piece of cheese. Hands seemed to revive after swallowing several deep gulps of brandy.

"Aye," he said, "by thunder, but I wanted some o'that!" Then he asked Jim what he was doing aboard.

"Well," said Jim, "I've come to take possession of this ship and you'll regard me as your captain until further notice."

With that, the boy set to work, hauled down the cursed Jolly Roger and chucked it overboard. Hands revived slowly and offered a bargain to Jim: if Jim gave him some food and some drink and something to tie up his wound, he would show Jim how to sail. Jim agreed—with one stipulation. He wanted to anchor in the North Inlet. In three minutes the *Hispaniola* was sailing easily, Hands's wounds were soon bound up, and Jim was greatly elated.

Hands told Jim how to lay the ship to and, after many tries, the boy finally succeeded and they sat down together to share a meal. Hands talked about O'Brien's body and about the possibility of dumping it overboard, then he asked for a bottle of wine. Brandy, he said, was too strong for his head; perhaps Jim could step below and get some wine. Jim was just a boy, but he was quick to realize that, for some reason, Hands wanted him to leave the deck. He promised the coxswain some port, in order to conceal his suspicions, and scurried away. When he had mounted the forecastle ladder, he was able to watch Hands; the worst of his suspicions proved true.

Painfully rising up, Hands got a long knife out of a coil of rope and hid it in his jacket, then returned to his place against the bulwark. Jim quickly stole back to the cabin and grabbed up a bottle of wine. At least, he thought, Hands wouldn't try anything until they were safe in a sheltered place.

Jim was right. With Hands's instructions, Jim navigated the schooner through the long, narrow passage of the North Inlet. Breathlessly, the boy put the helm hard up and the *Hispaniola* swung and settled on the low wooded shore. Then, Jim suddenly looked around and there was Hands, half-way toward him, the knife in his right hand.

Hands leaped forward. Jim dodged and struck Hands across the chest with the tiller. Just forward of the main-mast, he stopped, drew a pistol and let the hammer fall. There was no flash nor was there a sound. Hands moved fast, but the boy's reflexes were quicker. He was deftly avoiding the coxswain's knife when the ship rolled over to the port side until the deck was at a forty-five degree angle. Both men were thrown forward, Jim springing into the mizzen shrouds and not drawing a breath until he was seated on the cross-trees. Quickly he changed the priming of his pistol and addressed Hands:

"One more step, and I'll blow your brains out!"

Hands stopped instantly. "I don't have no luck, not I," he said.

Jim was smiling, feeling triumphant, when something sang through the air like an arrow. The boy felt a blow, then a sharp pang. He was pinned by the shoulder to the mast. Suddenly his two pistols went off and, with a choked cry, Hands plunged headfirst into the water. He rose once to the surface in a lather of foam and blood, and then sank. As the water settled, Jim saw Hands's body lying huddled on the clean, bright sandy bottom. He felt sick. Hot blood was running over his back and chest, and Hands's knife, where it had pinned Jim's shoulder to the mast, burned like a hot iron. Actually, the knife had almost missed Jim and was holding him by a mere pinch of skin. The boy gave a violent shudder and tore himself loose, tacked to the mast now only by his coat and shirt. Giving a sudden jerk, he wrenched himself free.

On land again, Jim headed for the area where he had encountered Ben Gunn. Dusk had come and he could not see well, but he did notice a wavering glow against the sky. Someone was cooking supper before a roaring fire.

Gradually the night became pitch-black, except for a glimmer on top of Spy-glass. Jim skirted the camp and, nearing the stockade, he was puzzled by the remains of an immense fire. It had not been the captain's habit to build fires. He began to fear that something had gone wrong while he was absent. Crawling on his hands and knees, he reached the door. He crept in and his foot struck something—a sleeper's leg.

A shrill voice broke the silence: "Pieces of eight! pieces of eight! pieces of eight! pieces of eight!"

It was Silver's green parrot, Cap'n Flint! Jim had no time to recover. He turned to run and was caught by strong arms which held him tight.

"Bring me a torch!" he heard. The voice belonged to Silver.

## PART VI

### Captain Silver

The red glare of the torch revealed a frightening sight. The pirates had taken possession of the house — and there was not a sign of a prisoner. With a heavy heart, Jim presumed that his friends were most likely dead. There were six pirates, all drunk, and Long John Silver, his parrot preening herself on his shoulder. Silver puffed on his pipe and lectured Jim on mischief. The doctor and the captain, he said, were furious with young Hawkins. (Jim was relieved: his friends *were* alive!) Now, would Jim join Silver's crew? Jim asked for information about his friends and was told that when they saw that the ship was gone, they bargained with Silver for food, brandy, and firewood and went to another part of the island.

"Silver," Jim said, "you are in a bad way: your ship lost, the treasure lost, your men lost; your whole business gone to wreck; and if you want to know who did it — it was I!" He elaborated on his schemes and said that he had nothing to fear.

No one spoke, then Morgan went for a knife. Silver stopped him, the two seamen quarreled, then Silver threatened the men: *he* was the captain; they would obey him — unless they wanted to see the color of their insides. Pointing to Jim, he said that the boy was more of a man than any of them; they were "rats." Furthermore, if anyone laid a hand on Jim, they would have to answer to Silver himself. There was a long pause, then the men trooped out of the house, muttering that they had their rights and were going outside for a council. Silver and Hawkins were left alone.

The sea-cook removed his pipe and confided to Jim that the crew were against them both, but that he would help Jim if Jim would save Silver from the gallows. Hawkins was bewildered, but he agreed to the bargain.

The council lasted some time. Jim looked out of one of the loopholes and saw the men huddling around the fire. He noted the gleam of a knife blade and what he thought was a book, though he wondered how anything so incongruous had come into their possession.

When the men returned, one of their group came timidly forward and handed Silver a small piece of paper. As the sea-cook expected, it was the "black spot," and the book that they had cut it out of was the Bible. Silver tried to shame the men and make light of the matter, but George Merry was firm. Silver, he said, had "made a hash of the cruise," had allowed Dr. Livesey and Squire Trelawney to escape, and then there was the matter of Jim—"this here boy." The men were vehement, but Silver countered: the boy was a hostage. Before the cruise, Squire Trelawney had instructed that a ship be dispatched if the squire had not returned by a set date. And why did Silver bargain with the squire? for food; if he hadn't, they'd all be starving. Then Silver dramatically cast before them the treasure map. The men were stunned. Once more they were ready to follow Long John.

Next morning Jim was awakened by Dr. Livesey's voice. The doctor, after receiving Silver's permission, entered the mutineers's camp and tended to the men. He betrayed no apprehension. He rattled on to his patients as if he were paying an ordinary professional visit to an ordinary English household. Dick, the doctor said, had malaria—due to Silver's camping in a bog.

Before he left, Livesey asked to talk privately with Jim Hawkins. Outside, he begged the boy to try and escape, but Jim refused. He had given Silver his word not to try and run for it. Then he told the doctor about the *Hispaniola*, lying in the North Inlet where Jim had beached her. The doctor was overjoyed and, shaking hands with Jim, set off at a brisk pace into the woods.

Later, when Silver was alone with Jim, he confided that he was aware that Livesey had tried to tempt the boy to escape. He commended Jim for his loyalty and emphasized that the two of them should stick close and save their necks "in spite of fate and fortune."

After a hearty meal, the mutineers set off in earnest to hunt for the treasure. Silver led the band, a pistol in each pocket of his square-tailed coat; behind him, at the end of a rope about his waist, was Jim.

A tall tree was the principal mark they looked for first. Each man decided on a different tree, but Long John shrugged his shoulders and kept moving on. The part of the island they explored was most pleasant; flowering shrubs were abundant and there were many thickets of nutmeg trees. The men spread out, in a fan shape, and not long afterward they heard one of their crew cry out, loudly. When they reached the fellow, they saw what had frightened him—a human skeleton, with a few shreds of clothing, lay on the ground. Curiously, his feet pointed in one direction and his hands, raised above his head like a diver's, pointed directly in the opposite direction. To Silver, the skeleton was a compass, pointing E.S.E. by E. Of lesser importance was the fact that this was probably the remains of Allardyce, one of Flint's crew. There was little time for reflection; Silver was eager to be off. Yet the pirates no longer ran shouting through the woods; now they kept side by side and spoke softly.

When they reached the top of the steep plateau, they sat down, exhausted, and looked out over the vast view. Morgan mentioned the name of Flint again and the mood became death-quiet. Out of the silence of the woods came a high trembling voice:

"Fifteen men on the Dead Man's Chest—
Yo-ho-ho, and a bottle of rum!"

All color drained from the men's faces; some leaped to their feet, some grabbed hold of the others. Morgan groveled on the ground. Then the song stopped as suddenly as it began. Silver tried to calm his crew but he too had difficulty speaking. The high voice broke out again. Some one gasped, "Let's go." Dick had his Bible out and was praying loudly.

Silver suddenly had an inspiration. "It's Ben Gunn," he roared and it was extraordinary how their spirits revived. They shouldered their pickaxes and set forth again.

Silver soon began grunting, his nostrils standing out and quivering. He was sure that the treasure was nearby. They passed through a thicket and, not ten yards farther, they stopped. Before them was a great hole, recently dug, and at the bottom was the shaft of a pick broken in two and the boards of several packing cases. On one of the boards, branded with a hot iron, was the name *Walrus*—the name of Flint's ship. The treasure had been found—and stolen.

The buccaneers began to leap in the pit, pawing with their fingers, throwing out boards. Cursing, Merry pointed to Silver. It was Silver's fault—he knew about it all along. The men were easily convinced and stood on one side of the pit; Jim and Silver stood on the other. Merry was raising his arm, plainly meaning to lead an attack, when three musket shots were fired out of a thicket. Merry fell headfirst into the hole, another spun around and fell down, twitching, and the other three fled in terror.

With smoking muskets, the doctor, Gray, and Ben Gunn joined Silver and Jim. As they were walking, the doctor related what had happened, about Ben's finding the skeleton *and* the treasure, which was in his cave. For that reason, the doctor had traded the map for their freedom.

When at last they reached the boats, the doctor smashed one of them with his pickaxe, then they set out for the North Inlet, a distance of eight or nine miles. They saw the squire, high on the two-pointed hill and hailed him; then, just inside the mouth of the North Inlet, they met the *Hispaniola*. The last flood had lifted her. They re-anchored her and headed for Gunn's cave. It was a large airy place, with a little spring and a pool of clear water. The floor was sandy and before a big fire lay Captain Smollett. In a far corner were great heaps of coins and bars of gold.

Next morning, the first of many trips were made to the *Hispaniola* in order to load the gold. It was a strange collection— English, French, Spanish, Portuguese and even Oriental pieces, bored through the middle. Day after day this went on and, on the third night, the wind brought a noise of shrieking and singing. It was the mutineers, said the doctor. "All drunk," said Silver.

When the gold was finally loaded and the anchor pulled up, the flag of the *Hispaniola* was raised once again. They were going home! They passed through the narrows and, very near the southern point, they saw the three cowardly mutineers, kneeling together, their arms raised in supplication. Seeing that the ship was not going to stop, one of them leaped to his feet and fired, the shot whistling over Silver's head.

The captain lay on a mattress in the stern and gave orders for the return voyage. They were heading for the nearest port in South America. Just at sundown, they cast anchor in a landlocked gulf and were immediately surrounded by boats full of Negroes and Mexicans and Indians.

Silver, Jim tells us, escaped in the confusion—but did not go empty-handed. He had cut through a bulkhead, unobserved, and had removed one of the sacks of coins. Jim says, however, that no one seemed particularly concerned: "I think we were all pleased to be so cheaply quit of him."

It has not been a pleasant memory that he has related—this tale of Treasure Island—and nothing could ever bring him back there. He still has nightmares and hears the surf booming and the ghostly high cry of Silver's parrot:

"Pieces of eight! pieces of eight!"

# CRITICAL INTERPRETATION

Stevenson began writing *Treasure Island* when he was challenged by his teen-age stepson to "write something really interesting." This perhaps is the real key to the novel. Stevenson deliberately composed a story that was fast-moving and adventurous, one that would entertain. The novel has no "secret symbols" or ambiguous meanings. It is simply a good narrative about a daring young boy, buried treasure, and pirates.

The novel was written rather quickly, the author often turning out a chapter a day. Afterward, he would read it aloud to his family. In fact, he would often consult his father about small details which would make the novel more authentic. Old Mr. Stevenson was very fond of this story of buried treasure and was a good source of information; he was a lighthouse engineer and had a vast knowledge of ships. It was he who suggested that an apple barrel would be a good place for Jim to hide in and overhear the mutineers.

Much of the novel's popularity is due to its first-person point of view. Jim Hawkins tells the story and because he says "I felt for the first time . . ." and "I saw great heaps of coins and bars of gold . . ." we respond emotionally. We identify with Jim's sense of wonder; we feel Jim's sharp pain when he is pinned by a knife to the cross-tree. This emotional response and identification is what every author hopes for.

Besides using a first-person point of view to catch our interest, Stevenson also filled his novel with what is often referred to as "atmosphere." In the first part of the novel, particularly, there is a sense of gloom and mystery. The old nut-brown sailor appears from out of nowhere; he has a heavy sea-chest that he guards suspiciously and he seems to be hiding, afraid of being found by a one-legged sailor. In addition, the setting is wintertime. The nights are stormy, the surf roars along the cove and up the cliffs, and the fog is thick and frosty. The names of the seamen—Black Dog and Billy Bones—emphasize that these are the "bad guys," the villains; Pew is blind and has a grip like a vice, Black Dog has two fingers missing, and Bones has a saber cut across one cheek. Stevenson is not subtle in these descriptions: these men were meant to be the epitomy of the vicious pirates that people so feared in those days. And Long John Silver himself: there is no other pirate in literature to match him. His wooden leg, his temper, and his shrill-voiced parrot make him almost inhuman.

The action in *Treasure Island* is lightning-quick. Some new complication occurs on almost every page, and the chapters are very short. We are never bored with paragraphs of superfluous descriptions; the novel never seems to be embroidered with its style. It is, throughout, lean and clear.

Stevenson has often been criticized for never attempting a serious masterpiece. But the romance and magic of *Treasure Island* and *Kidnapped* and *Dr. Jekyll and Mr. Hyde* are timeless. They are exactly what Stevenson's stepson was asking for: "something really interesting."

## QUESTIONS FOR REVIEW

1. What is the "real name" of Treasure Island, according to Long John Silver?

2. What is the "black spot"?

3. What is the name of Silver's inn and also the name of the highest hill on Treasure Island?

4. What is Silver's job on the *Hispaniola*?

5. Why doesn't Smollett want to captain the voyage?

6. Where is Jim when he hears Silver discussing the mutiny?

7. Describe Israel Hands's death.

8. Why is Ben Gunn on Treasure Island?

9. What is the Union Jack?

10. Besides Jim Hawkins, who else narrates the novel?

11. Who is Silver's parrot named after?

12. Describe "Jolly Roger."

13. How large is Treasure Island?

14. What happens to Long John Silver?

15. How many of the original crew return to Bristol?

# Kidnapped

## LIST OF CHARACTERS

**Alexander Balfour**

David's father; a schoolmaster.

**Mr. Campbell**

Minister of Essendean.

**David Balfour**

A sixteen-year-old lad who sets out to seek his fortune.

**Jennet Clouston**

Said to be something of a witch; curses old Ebenezer Balfour.

**Elias Hoseason**

Captain of the *Covenant.*

**Mr. Rankeillor**

Lawyer in Queensferry.

**Ransome**

A cabin-boy aboard the *Covenant.*

**Mr. Shuan**

Chief mate aboard the *Covenant.*

**Mr. Riach**

A small man of about thirty; hot-tempered and moody.

**Alan Breck Stewart**

Brave, somewhat pompous rebel; friend and confidant of David.

**Duncan Stewart**

Alan's father.

**Ardshiel**

Exiled captain of Alan's clan.

**James Stewart**

Ardshiel's half-brother.

**The "Red Fox"**

Colin of Glenure; a fierce, revenge-seeking Campbell.

**Hector Maclean**

A Highland money changer.

**Sheamus**

James of the Glens' agent.

**Duncan Mackiegh**

A wily blind catechist whom David meets on the way to Torosay.

## Neil Roy Macrob

Skipper of the ferry that travels between Torosay and Kinlochaline.

## Henderland

A wandering catechist.

## John Breck Maccoll

A savage-looking man who carries a message to James Stewart's wife.

## Cluny Macpherson

One of the chief rebels of the great uprising in 1745.

## Duncan Dhu Maclaren

Host who cares for David during his month-long convalescence.

## Robin Oig

A hot-tempered piper.

## Torrance

Servant to Mr. Rankeillor.

## "Mr. Thompson"

Pseudonym for Alan Breck Stewart.

# SUMMARIES

## CHAPTERS I-VI

Early one June morning in 1751, David Balfour locked his father's house and set out on the road. He was sixteen, his parents were dead, and he had no idea where he was going. But he had made up his mind that his life would not begin and end in the little town of Essendean; the world was large and David wanted to see as much of it as he could. It was a good morning for leaving—the sun was warm, the birds were whistling in the lilac bushes, and the mist in the valley was lifting. David's spirits were high. Yet he had not passed through the garden gate until he was stopped. Mr. Campbell, the minister of Essendean, was waiting for him. Campbell was a kindly man; he asked if David had had breakfast and offered to walk as far as the ford with David.

As they walked, the minister told David that he had a letter for him, a letter written by David's father when he was gravely ill. It was to be given to David after "the house was redd up and the gear disposed of." The letter instructed David to go to the house of Shaws, not far from Cramond. There David's father had grown up and there David should return, for Balfour of Shaws was an honest and reputable family and could help David. The minister urged David to go; the journey would take about two days and if David's "high relations" should put him out, he would always have a home with the minister.

Sitting down on a big boulder, Mr. Campbell gave David some parting advice. He described what David might find in the "great house" and warned him to be obedient and slow to take offence. Remember, he warned, David had had a country rearing and the laird (lord) of the house must be obeyed. He then gave David a little packet containing a small Bible, a shilling piece, and a recipe for "Lilly of the Valley Water." This essence, if distilled and "cured" in an anthill for a month, would restore speech, comfort the heart, strengthen the memory and, like-wise, was good for sprains and the cholic.

Mid-morning on the second day of David's journey, he topped a hill and was startled to see, far below him, the sea and, smoking like a mighty oven, the city of Edinburgh. The sight brought his "country heart into his mouth." Soon he encountered a shepherd and got rough directions for the neighborhood of Cramond and, before long, he came out on the Glasgow road. A little farther on, he began to inquire about the house of Shaws — a name that was obviously not popular. Indeed, the neighbors seemed to hate and fear any mention of the house of Shaws. And Ebenezer Balfour, David's uncle, was "nae [no] kind of a man, nae kind of a man at all," according to a travelling barber.

This was a blow to David's illusions, but his heart sank further when he met Jennet Clouston on the road. She was a stout, sour-looking woman and when she pointed out the house of Shaws, her face lit up with malignant anger. She "spit on the ground and cracked her thumb at it" — that is, she put a curse on the family, which she did, "for the twelve hunner and nineteen time." The woman seemed as wild as a witch and David's courage faltered.

The sun had gone down when the lad reached the ruin-like house. The main entrance had never been finished, nor had one wing of the house. Many of the windows were broken and bats flew in and out. He heard someone rattling dishes, but there was no sound of speech — only a dry cough that came in fits. Cautiously he knocked, waited, then knocked again. Nothing stirred but the bats overhead. Then David panicked and began to kick and pound on the nail-studded door, shouting loudly for Mr. Balfour. He was about to run when he heard a cough overhead and, looking up, he saw a man's head in a tall nightcap and the mouth of a gun barrel pointing at him.

He explained about the letter and when he introduced himself as David Balfour, the old man paused a long time, then said that he would allow David to come inside.

After a great rattling of chains and bolts, David was taken into the kitchen, the barest room he had ever seen. As for Uncle Ebenezer, he was narrow-shouldered and stooped, his face was clay-colored, and his age might have been anything between fifty and seventy. He had not shaved for a long time.

David was given a bowl of porridge and while he ate it, his uncle stooped near the fire; he read the letter, then turned it over and over in his hands. The old man was clearly upset and David quickly assured him that he looked for no favors from his uncle; he was no beggar and if he was not welcome here, he had friends he could return to. Ebenezer paid little attention to his nephew's spirit; clearly he was thinking of other things.

Lighting no lamp, he set out into a dark passage, saying that it was time for bed. David stumbled after him and was pushed into a small room and, before he could protest, he heard the key turn. He was locked in—though in what, he wasn't sure. The bed was damp and mouldy, so David slept on the floor that night, rolled up in a blanket.

Next morning, during a breakfast of beer and porridge, the boy and his uncle talked a bit. Again David emphasized that he had too much pride to beg any favors from relatives that he'd never seen before; it was by no will of his own that he had sought out his uncle. Ebenezer's eyes played hide and seek with David, reinforcing the boy's distrust of the old man.

Later in the day, when he was examining some books, David came upon a puzzling inscription. On the flyleaf of one of the books was written: "To my brother Ebenezer on his fifth birthday." This was odd because, according to Ebenezer, David's father was the younger of the two. Yet the handwriting was excellent. When David asked his uncle about his brother's learning, Ebenezer didn't guess the reason for his nephew's curiosity. "Alexander," he said, "was not very quick." This puzzled David even more. Were Alexander and Ebenezer twins?

This question brought the old man to his feet. He caught David by the jacket, his eyes bright and blinking. Very calmly

David told his uncle to release him; he knew he was far stronger than the old man and did not frighten easily. (Yet was his uncle insane? If so, he truly might be dangerous.)

That night, after the table had been cleared, Ebenezer confessed to David that long ago he had promized Alexander to keep a bit of money for the boy. This he had done and the money was intact but was in a chest at the top of a stair-tower at the far end of the house. Pulling out a rusty key, he told David that the stairs were good and that besides money in the chest, there were also important papers.

Outside the wind was moaning and there was such a wild flash of lightning that David was half-blinded when he stepped into the tower. He edged his way up the stone steps and, knowing full well that he had five stories to go, he was grateful for a second fearful flash of lightning: the steps, he saw, were of unequal length and one of his feet rested within two inches of the stairwell. Getting down on his hands and knees, fighting off bats, David crawled upward. He was making a turn when his hand slipped. The stairs went no higher! He broke out in a cold sweat, turned carefully back, and half-way down, the rain began to fall in torrents. At the bottom, he looked out, toward the kitchen. The door was open and a figure was standing in the rain. There was an ear-splitting clap of thunder, and the old man ran into the house, where he seized a bottle and drank down great gulps of raw liquor. David stepped forward and clapped down his two hands on his uncle's shuddering shoulders.

Ebenezer gave a kind of broken sheep's cry and tumbled to the floor. David grabbed the keys hanging in the cupboard and began opening chests, hoping to find a gun before his uncle regained consciousness. His search was unsuccessful, but he did find a rusty knife which he concealed inside his waistcoat. Returning to his uncle, he dashed water in his face. Then he sat him on a chair and looked at him. Why had he tried to kill David? Why had he been afraid to discuss Alexander? Perhaps in the morning there would be some answers. He locked the old man in his room, pocketed the key and bedded down before a big fire, "a blaze as had not shone there for many a long year."

When David released his uncle next morning he was almost jeering: he was no "country Johnny Raw, with no more mother-wit or courage than a porridge-stick." Ebenezer murmured something about a bit of fun, but was interrupted by a knocking at the door. On the doorstep was a half-grown boy in sailor's clothes. He had a wierd look in his eyes and was snapping his fingers and doing a strange kind of dance. He had a letter, he said, for Mr. Balfour.

After Ebenezer had read the message, he told David that they would have to go to Queensferry in order to tend to business with Elias Hoseason, captain of the *Covenant;* in addition, they could talk to a lawyer, Mr. Rankeillor, about David's future. David pondered the proposition. In such a busy place as the docks his uncle was not likely to attempt violence; besides, he did need to see a lawyer. And, most important, perhaps, David did want to get a better look at the sea and ships. They would go to the city.

The little cabin-boy accompanied David and his uncle and talked most of the way, telling them that he'd been at sea since he was nine years old. He had tatoos, could swear horribly, and boasted of many wild things that he had done — including murder. He talked of the *Covenant's* captain, but said that he was no seaman. The finest seaman, he said, was Mr. Shuan and this he said despite the raw, red wound on his leg which Mr. Shuan was responsible for. The wound was terribly ugly. David felt his blood run cold. The little cabin-boy rattled on about the continual peril of his life, not merely from the wind and the sea, but from the cruelty of those who were his masters. But there were compensations: he had a rope of his own and "when they [the crew] carried little uns, he'd wallop them."

When they at last reached the pier, there was much bustle. The sailors were singing, but their songs did not lighten David's heart. He looked at the *Covenant* "with extreme abhorrence," pitying "all poor souls that were condemned to sail on her."

As soon as they came to the inn, Ransome, the cabin-boy, led them to the captain — a tall, dark, sober-looking man. He was wearing a thick sea-jacket and was sitting at a table, writing. David had never seen any man, not even a judge, look cooler or more studious and self-possessed than this sea-captain.

Thinking back, David knows now that he should never have let his uncle out of sight, but he was young then and he wanted a closer look at the sea. When he was told to "run down-stairs and play awhile," he did just that.

The smell of the sea was wild, salty and stirring; the *Covenant* was shaking out her sails and David daydreamed of far voyages and foreign places. Returning to the inn, he talked a bit to the landlord and asked if he knew Mr. Rankeillor, the lawyer. The landlord not only talked about Mr. Rankeillor but he also talked about Ebenezer Balfour. Rumor had it that the old man had killed his brother just to get the estate, for Alexander was the *elder*—not the younger—son. Of course, David says, he had thought about such a thing some time ago, but it is one thing to guess, another to know. He was stunned.

When David returned to the pier, Captain Hoseason hailed him. He told the boy that his uncle had said many good things about the lad. Would David like to come aboard the *Covenant*, inspect it himself, and have a drink with the captain? David was reluctant—he had an appointment with a lawyer—but the captain passed his arm through the boy's arm and said that he would see that David made it back to Rankeillor's. At that, David didn't dream of hanging back; the captain seemed to be a good man and David was overjoyed that he would have the opportunity to explore a ship.

The little skiff with David, his uncle, and the captain shoved off and, when they were alongside the brig, the captain was brought on board by lowering a tackle. Then it was David's turn. The boy was whipped into the air and set down on the deck. He was a little dizzy and a bit afraid.

"Where is my uncle," he asked suddenly. He felt lost. He ran to the railing and saw the skiff, pulling for town, with his uncle sitting in the stern. David cried for help and his uncle turned around, his face full of cruelty and terror. Strong hands pulled David back and a thunderbolt seemed to strike him. He saw a flash of fire and fell senseless.

## CHAPTERS VII-XIII

When David came to, he found himself in darkness, in great pain, and bound hand and foot. He was almost deafened by the roaring of heavy sprays, the thundering of the sails, and the shrill cries of seamen. A blackness of despair swept over him and he lost consciousness. Recovering, he was shaken by the same uproar and was nauseated by the ill-smelling cavern of the ship's bowels. Again he lost consciousness.

At length, he was awakened by the light of a hand-lantern, held by a small man with green eyes and a tangle of straw-colored hair. He let his wounds be washed and dressed but could not talk; he tried but all he could utter were sobs. The small man, Mr. Riach, proved to be a friend. Because he was insistent, he convinced the captain that David should be moved to the forecastle, where the other seamen had berths. David lay there for many days, listening to tales of the sea, of pirates and of cruel deeds. Yet these men were not wholly bad, David says, for most of his money was eventually returned by the crew. Mr. Riach, in particular, seemed kind. He listened to David's story of misfortune and said that he would give paper, pen, and ink to the boy so that he could write to Mr. Campbell and also to Mr. Rankeillor about Ebenezer's cruelty.

Mr. Shuan, on the other hand, was wholly different; he had two moods: he was either kindly, meaning he was sober—or he was violent, meaning that he was drunk. The latter mood caused no one any particular trouble except Ransome, the cabin-boy. He would often beat the boy severely. In fact, one night, he was so violent that he unknowingly murdered the boy. Immediately, the captain summoned David; he would take Ransome's place as cabin-boy.

David was kept busy in his new post. He had to serve at meals, and all day long he brought liquor to the men. His bed was hard and cold and it was rare that he slept without interruption, for some one would always be coming from the deck for a drink. The food was plain, usually oatmeal porridge, but David was allowed to sample, occasionally, the ship's "treasure" – the pickles. Some cabin-boys might have been tempted to drink all day long, but David did not do so, despite the knowledge that soon he would be slaving alongside Negroes in the tobacco fields as a slave.

More than a week went by; some days the *Covenant* would make a little way; other days, the wind would be strong and drive her back. On the tenth afternoon, a thick, wet, white fog descended on the boat and hid one end of the ship from the other. David was serving Mr. Riach and the captain their supper that night when the ship struck something. They had run a boat down.

Hurrying out, David learned that they had cut a boat in two and that all the crew, except one man, had gone to the bottom. The survivor had been sitting in the stern, had been thrown into the air, and had caught hold of the brig's bowspirit. It seemed incredible that a man could have such luck and such agility. Yet when David saw him, the man looked as cool as the sea itself.

He was small, deeply sunburnt, and was heavily freckled and pitted; he was wearing a great-coat, which he took off, laying a pair of silver-mounted pistols on the table.

The captain was as curious as David was about this man: he was wearing a French soldier's coat and yet he spoke with a Scottish accent. Unabashedly, the stranger explained that he was a Jacobite on his way to France; the French ship – unlike the *Covenant* – failed to contact his small boat in the fog. He then took a money-belt from around his waist and offered the captain sixty guineas if he would take the stranger to Linnhe Loch. The captain unsuccessfully haggled but finally agreed to the bargain and went out rather hurridly.

When they were alone, the stranger asked for liquor and David was quick to run on deck and ask for the key. There he saw the captain and two officers in a conference. David drew nearer and listened. Mr. Riach was proposing that they get the stranger out of the round-house. The captain disagreed. If the stranger were in the round-house, he wouldn't have room to use his sword.

David was seized with fear and anger. These were treacherous, greedy men that he sailed with. He gathered his courage and approached the captain and asked for the key to the liquor cabinet. Riach spoke first: did David know where the firearms were kept? The captain assured Riach that David knew. He said that the fellow they had saved was dangerous and an enemy to King George; David would be of immense help if he could nonchalantly get a pistol or two and some powder. If he would do that, the captain promised, he would bear it in mind when they came to the Carolinas. Furthermore, they'd share the contents of the money-belt with David.

What was David to do? They were villains—they had kidnapped David and had killed poor Ransome. Should David assist with yet another murder? Yet how could he, a boy, and the young stranger hold a whole ship's company?

The Jacobite was eating his supper when David returned.

"Do ye want to be killed?" David asked. Then he explained that the crew was murderous, but that he would stand by the stranger, who introduced himself as Alan Breck Stewart. The two made plans immediately. Stewart wanted one door open in order to be able to face his enemies. Then he gave David a cutlass; next, he set the boy down to the table with a powder-horn, a bag of bullets, and several pistols to be readied for the attack. There were fifteen men against them, David said, but Stewart did not flinch. He told David to get in a bed where he would be close to the window; if they tried to enter by that way, or by the other door, David was to shoot. From that position, he could also control the skylight.

It was the captain who first approached the round-house. Alan challenged him immediately, saying that "the sooner the clash begins, the sooner ye'll taste this steel throughout your vitals." In a moment the captain was gone.

The wind was steady and the sails were quiet. David could hear the sound of muttering voices, then a clash of steel; the crew were dealing out the cutlasses. His heart beat like a bird's, quick and light. If only the fracus would begin.

It came all of a sudden. "That's him that killed the boy," David cried out. It was Mr. Shuan in the doorway. In a minute Alan had passed his sword through the murderer's body. Beyond the window David spied five men using an improvised battering ram to smash the door in. Wildly he shot into their midst. One of them cried out and the rest stopped, then ran. Turning, David saw Alan standing proudly, his sword dripping blood. Again it was quiet, then someone dropped softly on the roof. There was a single whistle, then a knot of men made a rush at the door and, at the same moment, a man leaped through the skylight. David gave a shriek and shot the fellow in the stomach, then wounded a second man in the thigh. Alan rousted the men at the doorway and passed his sword through the dead and dying seamen on the floor. There was a flush on his face and his eyes were as bright as a child's at Christmas. Shortly he burst out with a Gaelic song. For David, however, the moment was not one of explosive joy. It was a nightmare and he began to sob and cry.

Alan commended the boy for his bravery, then bedded him down for three hours. When it was time for David to stand watch, absolute quiet had descended on the ship. The new day dawned and rain fell, although the sea was smoothly rolling. David was not at peace: blood ran to and fro amidst the broken glass on the round-house floor.

At breakfast, about six o'clock, Alan and David discussed their situation. Altogether, it was not too bad. They had rousted the officers from their cabin and had at their command all the liquor in the ship and, as Alan said, "you can keep a man from fighting, but never from his bottle." They were good company; Alan was proud and pleased with his new friend and as a token of friendship, he cut off one of the silver buttons from his coat and gave it to David. "Wherever you go," he said, "show that button and friends of Alan Breck will come around you."

Later in the morning, Mr. Riach requested a conference for the captain. David was suspicious, but Alan agreed to meet with Hoseason at one of the windows. Despite the pouring rain, the captain came for the appointment and stood in the rain and said that he hadn't enough men to sail his ship. He would have to put back into port at Glasgow. Alan refused and offered the captain again the sixty guineas if he would dock in the Linnhe Loch. It would risk the brig and the crew, but the captain said that he would attempt the landing. They closed the bargain by exchanging a bottle of brandy for two buckets of water.

During the early part of the day, Alan and David smoked a pipe or two of the captain's fine tobacco and exchanged stories. This was fortunate, for David learned some things about the wild Highland country on which he was soon to have many an adventure.

Alan confessed that he was a deserter from the English army, a fact that astonished David; desertion was punishable with death. Furthermore, Alan was a member of the French army, but had returned to Scotland every year since 1746, the year following the Jacobite uprising. His mission was dangerous but necessary. He returned to pick up recruits to serve France but, more important, he carried the forbidden rents for the banished Ardshiel. David was amazed at the generosity of the poor Highlanders; they paid one rent to the English king and another to their chief.

Alan told David about a certain Campbell, Colin of Glenure, the so-called Red Fox. As soon as Ardshiel was driven from the country, Colin had arranged to be the King's factor on the lands of Appin, and as soon as he heard of the rents sent overseas to Ardshiel, he declared all the farms under him were for rent. The country people, however, managed to out-bid all the Campbells. Red Fox was not beaten, though; since he couldn't be "rid of the loyal commons by fair means, he swore he would be rid of them by foul." So he "sent for lawyers, and papers, and red-coats to stand at his back. And the kindly folk of that country had to pack and tramp, every father's son out of his father's house." He didn't care that King George was thus denied rents; his goal was to hurt Ardshiel.

It was late at night when Hoseason appeared at the round-house door: the ship was in trouble. Alan did his best to help, as did Mr. Riach, who climbed aloft and shouted down directions for bypassing the long length of dangerous reefs. The way was perilous but eventually they emerged and were congratulating one another when the tide caught the *Covenant*. She came around into the wind like a top, and the next moment she struck a reef with such force that they were thrown flat upon the deck. A massive wave lifted the ship and David was cast up and into the sea. The country lad had no knowledge of swimming but after an hour of kicking and splashing, he reached a quiet, shallow piece of the sea and waded ashore.

## CHAPTERS XIV-XXX

It was past midnight and a cold wind was blowing when David reached shore. He took off his shoes and walked barefoot along the coast, beating his chest to stimulate circulation. There was no sound of man or even cattle; only the surf broke in the distance. David paced the beach until daybreak then he began climbing a rugged, granite cliff. There was no sign of the *Covenant* or the skiff.

He set off along the south coast, hoping to find a friendly house. Instead, after some time he realized that he was on a barren little isle, cut off on every side by the sea. A thick mist descended and rain soon followed. He walked for a while, shivering, then flung himself down on the sand and wept.

The time that David spent on the island is still so horrible to remember, he tells us, that he must pass it lightly over. He was ill a good deal of the time. His diet was of shellfish, eaten raw, which may have caused his miserable retching. Perhaps what made his solitude so horrible was the sight of an ancient church and many rooftops across the bay. And it rained until the afternoon of the third day. On that particular day, David sighted a small boat. He shouted and raised his hands and, although the men called out (in Gaelic) and laughed, they sailed past him.

On the following day, the boat returned and despite the sound of the breakers and his ignorance of Gaelic, David caught the word "tide" and noted that one of the men was waving his hand toward the mainland. Suddenly the meaning was clear. David ran back the way he had come and dashed across a stretch of sand that was covered with only a trickle of water. With a shout, he reached the main island.

The Ross of Mull, the main island, was rugged—all bog, briar, and big stones. David set out toward the smoke he had seen from the little island and, about five o'clock in the evening, he reached a low, longish cottage, roofed with turf and built of unmortared stones. On a mound in front of it, an old man sat, smoking his pipe in the fading sunlight.

The old man didn't know much English but David did understand that his shipmates had got safely ashore. One man in particular was dressed like a gentleman: Alan was safe! And, said the old gentleman, David was supposed to seek out Alan's country, by Torosay.

The next day David was on the road again and there he met other wandering folks, beggars mostly. He hired a guide who had difficulty, the farther they went, speaking English. His memory, however, quickened when David offered him money. Eventually greed overcame the fellow and he drew a knife on David, who trounced him thoroughly.

David's next "guide" was blind and carried a pistol. He questioned the boy about the money he carried and became so obnoxious and threatening that David told him that he too had a pistol and if the man didn't "strike across the hill due south," he would blow his brains out.

At Torosay, David inquired of an innkeeper if he was familiar with Alan Breck. Unhappily, the man bore some grudge against the family, but because he was drunk, he seemed harmless enough. That night, bedded down in a comfortable inn, David felt happy. His health had returned and his spirits were good.

The ferry trip from Torosay to the mainland was slow, but David enjoyed the songs and the sea air and the good nature of the passengers and the bright weather. He recalls only one melancholy interlude. In the mouth of Loch Aline, a gigantic ship was anchored and on shore and on board the ship, people were mourning and crying. It was clear that this was an emigrant ship bound for the American colonies. David shuddered, remembering that he too was once destined for America as a slave.

On the mainland, after cautiously inquiring about Alan Breck Stewart, David learned that a good deal of ferrying would be involved, for the sea in that part of the country ran deep into the mountains, winding and turning erratically. He was warned to avoid any Campbells and the "red-soldiers" and was advised to spend the night in an inn before setting out. This he did and next morning he was on the road, but in a short while he met another catechist. This fellow, Henderland, knew of Essendean's minister, Mr. Campbell. Campbell had translated into Gaelic a number of hymns and pious books which Henderland held in high esteem.

The journey was thus quite pleasant; Henderland was a likeable man and easy to talk with. David asked about the Red Fox and the Appin tenants and learned, unexpectedly, that Alan Breck was almost a mythic figure. "He's here and awa," said Henderland, "here today and gone tomorrow: a fair heather cat. He might be glowing [looking] at the two of us out yon bush, and I wouldn't wonder."

He said further that on the following day the expulsion of the tenants was to begin "under James's [James of the Glen, Ardshiel's half brother] very window." Theoretically there should be no trouble, but illegal firearms were hidden everywhere and the Red Fox was bringing soldiers with him.

David spent the night with Mr. Henderland and, next morning, arranged for a boat to take him farther on his travels. Ashore in Appin, he rested a bit in a birch wood growing on a steep, craggy side of a mountain and it was while he was sitting and thinking that he saw four travellers approaching. Rashly, the boy rose up from the bracken and asked the way to Aucharn. Fate could not have been more ironic; David was speaking to Colin Roy Campbell, the Red Fox. Campbell, however, had little time to question David, for from high on a hill came the sound of gunfire and the Red Fox fell from his horse, his head rolling on his shoulder: he was dead. David stood staring, horrified. Then he began to scramble up the hill, crying out, "the murderer! the murderer!" He spied a big man in a black coat and was running to catch him when a voice cried for him to halt. Campbell's men accused him of being an accomplice, posted by the road to hold them while the assassin took careful aim.

David's heart pounded. He felt helpless.

"Step in here, among the trees," said a voice, close by. It was Alan Breck, with a fishing rod. "Come!" he said, and the two began running until at last David collapsed on the forest floor.

It was not the old voice of friendship that Alan heard when the young boy had recovered sufficiently to speak. David, with his face still in the bracken, said that he and Alan must part. Murder had been done and Alan had been skulking in the trees. Alan swore he had no part in Red Fox's death, but David was not easily convinced. One thing, at least, was clear: Alan had exposed himself and David in order to divert the soldiers's attention from the murderer. The Highlander's defense was quick — he had performed an act of good Christianity; had Alan and David been the murderers, they'd be a good deal obliged if someone would have diverted the soldiers. David gave up trying to understand such logic and offered his hand in friendship.

After some talk about which direction to flee, Alan decided to attempt the vast area of heather, after a quick visit to his kinsman, James of the Glens, where he would get clothes and arms and money.

Night fell as they were walking and about half-past ten they saw the lights of a cottage. The door stood open and all around the house, carrying torches, scurried five or six persons. Alan whistled three times, in a particular manner, and at the sound of it, the moving torches came to a halt. At the yard gate, they were met by a tall, handsome man of more than fifty, who called out to Alan in Gaelic. Already James had heard of Red Fox's murder; it would bring trouble on the country. Meanwhile, the servants were digging in the thatch of the house, bringing forth guns and swords; none spoke above a whisper, but their voices sounded both anxious and angry.

While James talked with David in the kitchen, Alan took his bundle and went to the barn to change clothes and, afterward, David was given a change of clothing, including some Highland brogues made of deer leather. The two fellows were provided with swords and pistols, oatmeal, and a bottle of French brandy, and they quickly set out for the heather, heading eastward, and grateful for the mild dark night. Sometimes they walked, sometimes ran, passing huts hidden in quiet places of the hills. Half of the houses at which they stopped had already heard of the murder.

Daybreak found them in a deep valley with a turbulent, foaming river. Wild mountains stood all around and there was neither grass nor trees.

"This is no fit place," Alan commented and his understatement was accurate: it was a place that was bound to be watched. They ran to where the river split. Alan jumped to a rock in the middle of the stream, righted himself, then attempted to help

David. A deadly sickness of fear swept over the boy. Alan spoke, but the roaring of the falls was deafening. In a minute, the Highlander put the brandy bottle to the boy's lips and forced him to drink deeply: Turning, he leaped over the farther branch of the stream and was safe. David bent low on his knees and flung himself forward. His hands reached for a rock, slipped, caught, and slipped again. He was sliding back when Alan seized him, first by the hair, then by the collar, and with a great strain dragged him to safety. Without a word, they set off running, David sick and bruised and partly drunk from the brandy.

They stopped at the base of two rocks, some twenty feet high. On top, the rocks were somewhat hollow, making a kind of dish or saucer, with a protective over-hang. It seemed a godsend and they were quick to scramble to the place of safety. Alan offered to take the first watch, so David slept, grateful for the dry bracken bed.

When he awoke, the sky was cloudless and hot. About half a mile up the stream was a camp of red-coats and all the way down along the riverside were sentries. In fact, the entire valley was bristling with the flash of swords and sparkling red uniforms. All day long the two fugitives lay on the rock, "like scones upon a griddle." The sun beat down cruelly and all the while they had nothing to drink but warm brandy. At last, about two o'clock, the sun had moved a little into the west and a patch of shade fell on the east side of their rock, the side sheltered from the soldiers. At once they dropped on the ground and lay there for an hour or two. Then, shortly after sundown, they slipped from rock to rock until they reached the river. They plunged in, drank deeply and bathed until they ached with the chill. Finally refreshed, they began the ascent up the steep side of the mountains. The way was intricate but David managed it without much fatigue. Occasionally he would pause and look down, struck with wonder that he was so high — walking, it seemed, upon the clouds.

It was still dark when they reached their destination, a cleft in the head of a great mountain, with a stream running through and a shallow cave nearby. The name of the cleft was the Heugh of Corrynakiegh and it was a pleasant place for the five days they lived in it. They made themselves heather beds and cooked hot porridge, which was especially good with grilled trout.

It would be many a day, Alan said, before the red-coats would think of checking Corrynakiegh, but it would be wise to send word to James of the Glens. David had no idea how to send word, but Alan proved himself a wise and resourceful man. First, he fashioned a cross out of some wood, then he blackened the four ends of it with charcoal. He asked for the button which he had given to David and bound it on the cross, along with a little sprig of birch and one of fir. After dark, he explained, he would sneak down to a little town where lived a good friend of his, John Breck Maccoll. The fellow was none too bright but if his wits were about him when he discovered the cross in his window, he would reason that since the button belonged to the son of Duncan Stewart and was next to sprigs of birch and pine (a combination found in Corrynakiegh), then Alan was in the Heugh and was in need of help.

Alan's plan worked and about noon the next day a man appeared at their camp. He was ragged, wild, and bearded, and his face was disfigured by smallpox. He accepted the message which Alan wrote on a corner of his French military commission, and he said that he would make the trip as quickly as he could. He was gone for three days and it was about five in the evening when they heard a whistling in the woods. The fellow seemed less savage than before and well pleased to have finished such a dangerous mission. He gave them news of the countryside which was infested with red-coats and told them that many illegal arms had been found. In addition, James and some of his servants were already in prison at Fort William, under suspicion of complicity. It seemed that most people believed that Alan Breck had fired the shot that killed Red Fox; there was a reward issued for both him and David. Mrs. Stewart, Maccoll said, was ill and terribly melancholy and had enclosed only a small amount of money because it was all she could beg or borrow.

Maccoll returned the silver button to Alan, after a bit of badgering, and Alan promised to give him "the name of a good man" wherever he went. Alan and David quickly got their things together and resumed their flight.

After more than eleven hours of hard travelling, they arrived at the end of a range of mountains. In front of them lay a piece of low, broken desert land which they had to cross. A thin mist went up from the moorland. It would not be easy to cross the vast area, Alan warned, for if the red-coats came over a hill, they could spy them from miles away. They waited until the mist had disappeared and then they set out, David shuddering inside at the prospect of the endless dreary waste before him. The only sounds were the moorfowl and the peewees crying; far to the east a herd of deer moved like dots. Much of the moor was blood-red with heather, and the rest was broken up with bogs and peat pools. In another place there was a forest of dead firs, standing like skeletons. At least, however, it was clear of troops. At least, that is, it was free of soldiers until David awoke and saw a large body of soldiers approaching on horseback. When he did, he froze with fear and shame. He awakened Alan, explained that he had fallen asleep during his watch and told him what the situation was.

Alan was quick to react. They set off on their hands and knees, winding in and out of the lower parts of the moorland until they reached a big bush of heather and fell inside, panting and looking back to see if the dragoons had spotted them. They had not.

A heavy dew began falling when darkness descended on the moor and David was grateful; he was drenched but refreshed when they set out again. They walked all night, David following a pace or two behind, and were descending a heathery hill when the bushes gave a rustle and three or four men threw the two to the ground. They were in luck — it was Cluny's men. Cluny, Alan explained, had been one of the leaders of the great rebellion six years ago. The news seemed to come from far off; David's head buzzed and he felt light as a feather. He tried to walk, but was unable to, so two of the ragged fellows took him by the arms and led him through a labyrinth of dreary hollows and into the heart of Ben Alder mountain.

   Mounting a hillside, they found a strange house, referred to as "Cluny's Cage." A tree, which grew out from the hillside, was used as a center beam for the roof. The walls were covered with moss and the whole house had something of an egg shape; it half hung, half stood on the steep hillside like a wasp's nest. Within, it was large enough for five or six persons to live comfortably. A projection of the cliff had been used for a fireplace and, miraculously, the smoke rising against the face of the rock was not noticeable because the color of the rock was grey and smoke-like.

   This was but one of Cluny's hiding places, David learned; the renegade had caves and underground chambers in several parts of the country and, following the reports of his scouts, he moved from one to another as the soldiers drew near or moved away. Although he was stripped by an Act of Parliament of any legal powers, he nevertheless still exercised a patriarchal concern for his clan. Disputes were brought to him in his hiding-hole.

   Although he could be fierce, there was another side to Cluny: he loved to cook and, on the first day, he carefully prepared for David and Alan a magnificent dinner of venison scallops, which he dressed with a squeeze of lemon. When they were done eating, Cluny brought out an old, thumbed, greasy pack of cards. David protested that gambling and card-playing were games of the devil, but he was chided for being a stupid Whig and silenced. Seeing that his arguments were useless, he went to a corner of the Cage and lay down on a bed of heather. Then a strange heaviness came over him and soon he fell into a kind of trance, which lasted almost the whole time of their stay in the Cage.

   When David awakened on the third day, he saw Alan looking very downcast; he had lost all his money to Cluny, and David's money besides. While David was semi-conscious he had agreed to loan Alan money. David was furious, but Cluny quieted him finally by returning the boy's money.

   That night, the two set out again with one of Cluny's men for a guide. For a long time they said nothing to one another. They marched alongside each other, silent as stones. When they lay down to sleep, it was without a word. Alan was not pleased with this route, but he couldn't make David talk about it—despite the fact that this was enemy territory. David was bitter. Finally Alan could take it no longer and said that he would leave; this effected a reconcilliation. What he had always liked about David, he said, was that David never quarrelled, and "now I like ye better!"

When they arrived at a cottage owned by the Maclarens, David was put to bed and a doctor was called. It was not a good diagnosis; he lay bed-ridden for a week and it was a full month before he was able to take to the road again. All this time, Alan stayed nearby, hiding in the bushes and coming to the house at night to talk with his friend. Often they were entertained by Duncan Dhu (their host), who played for them on his pipes. In fact, the pipes proved to be the saving factor, perhaps, for Alan. Robin Oig, one of the sons of the notorious Rob Roy, came to the house one night to inquire about David and encountered Alan.

Because of an old quarrel, they were about to fight with swords when Duncan Dhu suggested pipes instead. Both proved to be expert musicians and played long into the night. It was the most beautiful music David had ever heard. Alan declared Robin to be the better piper and they parted good friends.

The month was not yet out, but it was already far into August and, fortunately, they had beautiful weather when David was pronounced ready to resume his journey. The first night they stayed with another family of Maclarens and then set forth again, sleeping in heather bushes, breathing fine, dry sunshine and before long Alan turned to David and announced that the boy was once again in his own land—almost. All that was left was to cross the river.

Despite the fact that they had no boat, Alan had a plan. They entered an inn and appealed to the serving girl's sympathy. David pretended to be a poor, sick, overwrought lad and Alan was his tender comrade; they needed a boat to cross to the other side of the river. The girl was touched immediately and brought them a dish of white puddings and a bottle of strong ale. Later that night, she rowed them across to safety.

The next day, while Alan hid in the fields by the roadside, David walked into Queensferry. The town was just beginning to awaken; fires were being kindled, windows were being opened, and the people were coming out of their houses. They looked askance at David, nudging one another with smiles. David glanced down at his rags and dirt, and hurried on until he chanced to stop in front of a fine house with a dog yawning on the steps. He was envying the dog when the door was opened and a ruddy-faced man in a well-powdered wig and spectacles came out. Because of David's poor appearance, he approached the lad and asked what he did. It was discovered that the very man whom David was seeking—Mr. Rankeillor, a lawyer for Ebenezer Balfour—was standing in front of the boy.

The lawyer took David into the house, looking worriedly at the boy's muddy rags, and sat him down in a small dusty chamber full of books and documents. He asked him about his early life and quizzed him a bit on the Latin he would have learned from Mr. Campbell, were he in fact David Balfour. Satisfied that this was the lad, the lawyer offered David some clean clothes and also some water and soap. Dinner would be served below.

David made what changes he could and was amazed when he looked in the mirror: he had come to life again. Mr. Rankeillor met him on the stairs, made his compliments, and asked David to talk with him before dinner. He told him a great deal about Uncle Ebenezer and about David's father, Alexander Balfour.

Once long ago Ebenezer had not been an ugly man. He had a fine, gallant air; people stood in their doors to watch him as he went by on horseback. Then, in 1715, he had run away to join the rebels. David's father pursued him, found him in a ditch, and brought him back. Then it chanced that the two lads fell in love with the same lady. There was much unhappiness in the Balfour house; Ebenezer screamed like a peacock and the whole country heard of the feud. But the Balfour brothers came to a bargain: David's father took the lady and Ebenezer took the estate. Those who knew the story gave Ebenezer a cold shoulder; those who knew it not, seeing one brother disappear, and the other succeed in the estate, raised a cry of murder. So, on all sides, Ebenezer found himself alone. Money was all he got by his bargain.

Now, about David's getting a share of the estate: lawsuits were expensive and always scandalous. But there was possibly one way, involving David's friend, "Mr. Thompson," as Mr. Rankeillor preferred to call Alan Breck. They both went to greet Alan, accompanied by Rankeillor's servant, Torrance, and as they walked to the house of Shaws, the lawyer explained his plan to "Mr. Thompson."

It was quite dark when they came in view of the house of Shaws. There was no glimmer of light. The lawyer and Torrance and David crept quietly up and crouched beside a corner of the house and, as soon as they were concealed, Alan strode to the door and began to knock.

It was some time before Alan's knocking brought a response. Then a window was jerked up and a voice demanded to know what was going on, and announced that he had a gun ready for any intruders. Alan said, without explanation, that he had come about the fate of young David. At the sound of that name, Ebenezer's voice changed. He agreed to come down and, with a creaking of hinges, the old uncle stepped gingerly onto the doorstep, his gun ready in his hands.

Alan explained that a ship had been lost in his area of Scotland and that one of his family, who was seeking wreck-wood for his fireplace, had come upon a lad who was half-drowned. He took the boy and kept him in an old, ruined castle where, from that day to this, he had been "a great expense." So the matter came to this: the boy said that his uncle, Ebenezer, had arranged for his kidnapping. Would Ebenezer pay a ransome for the boy or would he pay to have the boy killed? The old man was not for murder, but he did not want the boy back. He would pay a generous sum to have the boy kept in the castle. Alan persisted in questioning the old man and drew out of him additional information about the kidnapping. Ebenezer had paid Captain Hoseason twenty pounds to kidnap the boy. But, explained Ebenezer, Hoseason had the best of the bargain because he was to have all the profit from selling the boy in the Carolinas.

At that, Mr. Rankeillor stepped forth from the shadows. "Good evening, Mr. Balfour," he said.

"Good evening, Uncle Ebenezer," said David.

David's uncle said not a word; he just sat down on the doorstep and stared like a man turned to stone. Alan grabbed up the gun and the lawyer, taking the old man by the arm, led him into the kitchen. He promised him that they would make easy terms. In the meantime, he said, he wanted the cellar key so that Torrance could bring them up a good bottle of wine in honor of the event. Turning to David, he wished him all the joy and good fortune possible.

Next morning, Alan was much in David's thoughts and, after the lawyer and his servant had taken their farewell, David and his friend set out for the city of Edinburgh. As they walked along the footpath and passed the gateposts and the unfinished lodge, they kept looking back at the house of Shaws. They walked slowly forward, having little heart either to walk or speak. The same thought was in both of them; they were near the time for their parting. They did talk, however, and decided that Alan should keep to the country, staying now here, now there, but coming once a day to a particular place where David might be able to communicate with him, either in person or by messenger. In the meanwhile, David was to find a lawyer, who was an Appin Stewart, and a man who was to be wholly trusted and who would arrange for Alan's embarkation.

When they came to the place called Rest-and-be-Thankful, they stopped and looked over at the city. They both knew, without a word said, that they had come to where their ways parted.

David gave his friend what money he had, then they stood a while and looked over at Edinburgh in silence. Neither of them looked the other in the face when they offered their final good-byes. David felt lost and lonesome. He could have sat down and wept, but he did not. He went on his way into the city and was soon amidst the hubbub of Edinburgh.

## CRITICAL INTERPRETATION

A brief background on the Jacobite Revolution of 1745 helps one to understand why Alan Breck Stewart is so fiercely loyal to his clan and to Scotland. Alan was among many people in England—and Scotland—who were unhappy with King George. They wanted to be ruled by a Stuart and had not been since 1714. George, according to them, did not have sufficient claim to the throne; he had no Stuart blood-line. He became king as a result of political leaders deciding to give the throne to his father, the Elector of Hanover. Those citizens who hoped to restore a Stuart in the palace were called Jacobites (*Jacobus* being the Latin for *James*). This was no mere pipe-dream; these people were intensely loyal to the Stuarts, willing to die for their beliefs. In 1715, James Edward attempted to reclaim his father's kingdom and failed. Thirty years later, "Bonnie Prince Charlie," James's grandson initiated the bloody "Forty-Five," as the revolution was popularly called.

Like *Treasure Island,* this novel has a young man as its narrator and as its main character—or, actually, two young men (David Balfour and Alan Breck Stewart) as its main characters. And each of them, it is important to note, is more carefully created than Jim Hawkins was. Jim was the pivot of a good deal of action: he was scared when the occasion warranted it, ready to take chances, and inclined to be stubborn. The pirates were broadly drawn and so was Jim; they were "all bad," Jim was "all boy."

David, on the other hand, is older (he is sixteen) and Alan is a young adult. In addition, David has a keen sense of humor, a quality we rarely — if ever — discern in Jim Hawkins. David, for example, confesses to us how he smiled inwardly at Minister Campbell's recipe for "Lilly of the Valley Water"; obviously, the recipe was very dear to the old man — David should not jeer, even privately. Also he tells us about the pang of guilt which he felt when he left Essendean: Mr. Campbell was very sorry to see David go; David could barely wait to get away.

Especially when he is describing Alan, David tells us that he often felt like laughing at his new friend's pompous ways; he never did, of course, but because he finds Alan a bit too strutty and hot-headed, the Highlander is humanized. Long John Silver was merely an adventurer out for gold, ready to strike down any one in his way. Alan is responsible for transporting rents to his exiled chief, risking his life by returning to Scotland, yet he will not disguise himself. He is proud of his French finery and he refuses to cut off another button when he is fashioning the "message" for Maccoll: he asks David for the loan of the button with which he pledged everlasting friendship.

Because these two young men — opposites in religious and political beliefs — are such close friends, we can understand and sympathize when Stevenson slows down his narrative and concentrates on their quarrel, their long silences as they walk, and the anguish within each of them.

In general, this novel moves more slowly than *Treasure Island*. After David is on the mainland, he meets other travellers, rides ferries, and lies ill for some time. Stevenson uses this slower pace, however, to give us a sense of the Scottish Highlands — the peat bogs, the dreary moors, the craggy, steep mountains. And, also, we are introduced to the Highlanders themselves — a fiery people, ready to help you if you agreed with their cause or to curse or kill you if you disagreed.

When David Balfour left his small town, he little imagined that he would return a man who had survived vicious seamen, shipwreck, and near starvation — a man who would have witnessed murder and who actually had killed men himself. This, then, is the story of a young man's odyssey to maturity, how he founded a deep friendship and how he acquired a sense of self-reliance. The novel has never been as popular as *Treasure Island*; perhaps this is because of the great amount of dialect throughout, but, with patience, one discovers that it is a finer novel, its characters better developed and its psychology more mature.

## QUESTIONS FOR REVIEW

1. How old is David Balfour when he sets out to seek his fortune?

2. Describe Ebenezer Balfour and his house.

3. Which brother was older—Ebenezer or Alexander?

4. What is the name of Captain Hoseason's ship?

5. Discuss Alan Breck's coming aboard.

6. What are Hoseason's plans for David?

7. Why is Alan Breck returning to Scotland?

8. Who kills Ransome, the cabin-boy?

9. Describe the death of the "Red Fox."

10. What is a moor like? What are its features?

11. What is the fate of the *Covenant?*

12. Describe Alan's "message" to John Maccoll.

13. What is the psuedonym that Mr. Rankeillor uses when he refers to Alan?

14. Who is Cluny?

15. How does David finally manage to claim his inheritance?

# Selected Bibliography

BALFOUR, G. *The Life of Robert Louis Stevenson*. New York: Scribner, 1915.

BOK, E. W. "The Playful Stevenson," *Scribner's Magazine*, Aug. 1927, 82: 179-80.

BROWN, G. E. *A Book of R. L. S.* London: Methuen, 1919.

COOPER, L. U. *Robert Louis Stevenson*. Denver: Swallow, 1948.

DAICHES, DAVID. *Robert Louis Stevenson*. Norfolk, Conn.: New Directions, 1947.

FERGUSSON, A. S. "Stevenson the Dreamer," *Queens Quarterly*, July 1922, 30: 26-36.

QUILLER-COUCH, A. "Robert Louis Stevenson," *Adventures in Criticism*. New York: Putnam, 1925.

RICE, R. A. *Robert Louis Stevenson: How to Know Him*. Indianapolis: Bobbs, 1916.

# Study Smart with Cliffs StudyWare®

Cliffs StudyWare is interactive software that helps you make the most of your study time. The programs are easy to use and designed to let you work at your own pace.

**Test Preparation Guides—**
Prepare for major qualifying exams.
• Pinpoint strengths and weaknesses through individualized study plan. • Learn more through complete answer explanations. • Hone your skills with full-length practice tests. • Score higher by utilizing proven test-taking strategies.

**Course Reviews**—Designed for introductory college level courses.
• Supplement class lectures and textbook reading. • Review for midterms and finals.

| Qty. | Title | | Price | Total | Qty. | Title | | Price | Total |
|---|---|---|---|---|---|---|---|---|---|
| | Algebra I | ☐IBM ☐Mac | 19.98 | | | Science Bndl. (Biol., Chem., Physics) | | 34.98 | |
| | Algebra I CD-ROM (IBM & Mac) | | 19.98 | | | Statistics | ☐IBM ☐Mac | 19.98 | |
| | Biology | ☐IBM | 19.98 | | | Trigonometry (TMV) | ☐IBM ☐Mac | 19.98 | |
| | Biology CD-ROM (IBM & Mac) | | 19.98 | | | ACT | ☐IBM ☐Mac | 19.98 | |
| | Calculus | ☐IBM ☐Mac | 19.98 | | | ACT CD-ROM (IBM & Mac) | | 19.98 | |
| | Calculus CD-ROM (IBM & Mac) | | 19.98 | | | CBEST | ☐IBM ☐Mac | 19.98 | |
| | Chemistry | ☐IBM ☐Mac | 19.98 | | | College Bound Bndl. (ACT, SAT, U.S. News) | | 29.98 | |
| | Chemistry CD-ROM (IBM & Mac) | | 19.98 | | | GED | ☐IBM ☐Mac | 19.98 | |
| | Economics | ☐IBM ☐Mac | 19.98 | | | GRE | ☐IBM ☐Mac | 19.98 | |
| | Geometry | ☐IBM ☐Mac | 19.98 | | | GRE CD-ROM (IBM & Mac) | | 19.98 | |
| | Geometry CD-ROM (IBM & Mac) | | 19.98 | | | LSAT | ☐IBM ☐Mac | 19.98 | |
| | Math Bundle (Alg., Calc., Geom., Trig.) | | 39.98 | | | SAT I | ☐IBM ☐Mac | 19.98 | |
| | Physics | ☐IBM ☐Mac | 19.98 | | | SAT I CD-ROM (IBM & Mac) | | 19.98 | |

*Prices subject to change without notice.*

Available at your booksellers, or send this form with your check or money order to **Cliffs Notes, Inc., P.O. Box 80728, Lincoln, NE 68501** http://www.cliffs.com

*get the Cliffs Edge!*

☐ Money order   ☐ Check payable to Cliffs Notes, Inc.

☐ Visa   ☐ Mastercard   Signature _____

Card no. _____ Exp. date _____

Name _____

Address _____

City _____ State_____ Zip_____

GRE is a registered trademark of ETS. SAT is a registered trademark of CEEB.

1997

# Your Guides to Successful Test Preparation.

## Cliffs Test Preparation Guides
### • Complete • Concise • Functional • In-depth

Efficient preparation means better test scores. Go with the experts and use *Cliffs Test Preparation Guides*. They focus on helping you know what to expect from each test, and their test-taking techniques have been proven in classroom programs nationwide. Recommended for individual use or as a part of a formal test preparation program.

Publisher's ISBN Prefix 0-8220

| Qty. | ISBN | Title | Price | Qty. | ISBN | Title | Price |
|---|---|---|---|---|---|---|---|
| | 2078-5 | ACT | 8.95 | | 2044-0 | Police Sergeant Exam | 9.95 |
| | 2069-6 | CBEST | 8.95 | | 2047-5 | Police Officer Exam | 14.95 |
| | 2056-4 | CLAST | 9.95 | | 2049-1 | Police Management Exam | 17.95 |
| | 2071-8 | ELM Review | 8.95 | | 2076-9 | Praxis I: PPST | 9.95 |
| | 2077-7 | GED | 11.95 | | 2017-3 | Praxis II: NTE Core Battery | 14.95 |
| | 2061-0 | GMAT | 9.95 | | 2074-2 | SAT* | 9.95 |
| | 2073-4 | GRE | 9.95 | | 2325-3 | SAT II* | 14.95 |
| | 2066-1 | LSAT | 9.95 | | 2072-6 | TASP | 8.95 |
| | 2046-7 | MAT | 12.95 | | 2079-3 | TOEFL w/cassettes | 29.95 |
| | 2033-5 | Math Review | 8.95 | | 2080-7 | TOEFL Adv. Prac. (w/cass.) | 24.95 |
| | 2048-3 | MSAT | 24.95 | | 2034-3 | Verbal Review | 7.95 |
| | 2020-3 | Memory Power for Exams | 5.95 | | 2043-2 | Writing Proficiency Exam | 8.95 |

*Prices subject to change without notice.*

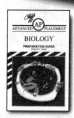

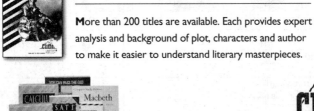

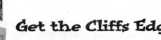